Truth may seem, but cannot be:
Beauty brag, but 'tis not she;
Truth and beauty buried be.

To this urn let those repair
That are either true or fair;
For these dead birds sigh a prayer.

Bacon

GEORGE ELIOT

BY

MATHILDE BLIND

NEW EDITION.

LONDON :

PRINTED BY WILLIAM CLOWES AND SONS, LIMITED,
STAMFORD STREET AND CHARING CROSS.

PREFATORY NOTE,

DETAILED accounts of GEORGE ELIOT'S life have hitherto been singularly scanty. In the dearth of published materials a considerable portion of the information contained in this biographical study has, necessarily, been derived from private sources. In visiting the places connected with GEORGE ELIOT'S early life, I enjoyed the privilege of meeting her brother, Mr. Isaac Evans, and was also fortunate in gleaning many a characteristic fact and trait from old people in the neighbourhood, contemporaries of her father, Mr. Robert Evans. For valuable help in forming an idea of the growth of GEORGE ELIOT'S mind, my warm thanks are especially due to her oldest friends, Mr. and Mrs. Charles Bray, and Miss Hennell of Coventry. Miss Jenkins, the novelist's schoolfellow, and Mrs. John Cash, also generously afforded me every assistance in their power.

A great part of the correspondence in the present volume has not hitherto appeared in print, and has been kindly placed at my disposal by Mrs. Bray, Mrs. Gilchrist, Mrs. W. K. Clifford, Miss Marks, Mr. William

M. Rossetti, and the late James Thomson. I have also quoted from letters addressed to Miss Phelps which were published in *Harper's Magazine* of March 1882, and from one or two other articles that have appeared in periodical publications. For permission to make use of this correspondence my thanks are due to Mr. C. L. Lewes.

By far the most exhaustive published account of GEORGE ELIOT'S life and writings, and the one of which I have most freely availed myself, is Mr. Call's admirable essay in the *Westminster Review* of July 1881. Although this, as indeed every other article on the subject, states GEORGE ELIOT'S birthplace incorrectly, it contains many important *data* not mentioned elsewhere. To the article on GEORGE ELIOT in *Blackwood's Magazine* for February 1881, I owe many interesting particulars, chiefly connected with the beginning of GEORGE ELIOT'S literary career. Amongst other papers consulted may be mentioned a noticeable one in the *Contemporary Review*, and an appreciative notice by Mr. Frederick Myers in *Scribner's Magazine*, as well as articles in *Harper's Magazine* of May 1881, and *The Century* of August 1882. Two quaint little pamphlets, 'Seth Bede: the Methody,' and 'George Eliot in Derbyshire,' by Guy Roslyn, although full of inaccuracies, have also furnished some curious items of information.

MATHILDE BLIND.

CONTENTS.

———◦◦◦———

PAGE

CHAPTER IX.

CHAPTER X.

CHAPTER XI.

CHAPTER XII.

CHAPTER XIII.

CHAPTER XIV.

CHAPTER XV.

GEORGE ELIOT.

CHAPTER I.

INTRODUCTORY.

SPEAKING of the contributions made to literature by her own sex, George Eliot, in a charming essay written in 1854, awards the palm of intellectual pre-eminence to the women of France. "They alone," says the great English author, "have had a vital influence on the development of literature. For in France alone the mind of woman has passed, like an electric current, through the language, making crisp and definite what is elsewhere heavy and blurred; in France alone, if the writings of women were swept away, a serious gap would be made in the national history."

The reason assigned by George Eliot for this literary superiority of Frenchwomen consists in their having had the courage of their sex. They thought and felt as women, and when they wrote, their books became the fullest expression of their womanhood. And by being true to themselves, by only seeking inspiration from their own life-experience, instead of servilely copying that of men, their letters and memoirs, their novels and pictures have a distinct, nay unique, value, for the student of art and literature. Englishwomen, on the other hand, have not followed the spontaneous impulses of nature. They have not allowed free play to the peculiarly feminine element, preferring to mould their intellectual products on the masculine pattern. For that reason, says George Eliot, their writings are "usually an absurd exaggeration of the masculine style, like the swaggering gait of a bad actress in male attire."

This novel theory, concerning a specifically feminine manifestation of the intellect, is doubly curious when one compares it with Madame de Staël's famous saying, "*Le génie n'a pas de sexe.*" But an aphorism, however brilliant, usually contains only one half the truth, and there is every reason to think that women have already, and will much more largely, by-and-by, infuse into their works certain intellectual and emotional qualities which are essentially their own. Shall we, however, admit George Eliot's conclusion that Frenchwomen alone have hitherto shown any of this original bias? Several causes are mentioned by her in explanation of this exceptional merit. Among these causes there is one which would probably occur to every one who began to reflect on this subject. The influence of the "Salon" in developing and stimulating the finest feminine talents has long been recognised. In this school for women the gift of expression was carried to the utmost pitch of perfection. By their active co-operation in the discussion of the most vital subjects, thought became clear, luminous, and forcible ; sentiment gained indescribable graces of refinement ; and wit, with its brightest scintillations, lit up the sombre background of life.

But among other causes enumerated as accounting for that more spontaneous productivity of French-women, attributed to them by George Eliot, there is one which would probably have occurred to no other mind than hers, and which is too characteristic of her early scientific tendencies to be omitted. For according to her, the present superiority of Frenchwomen is mainly due to certain physiological peculiarities of the Gallic race. Namely, to the "small brain and vivacious temperament which permit the fragile system of woman to sustain the superlative activity requisite for intellectual creativeness," whereas "the larger brain and slower temperament of the English and Germans are in the womanly organisation generally dreamy and passive. So that the *physique* of a woman may suffice as the substratum for a superior Gallic mind, but is too thin a soil for a superior Teutonic one."

So knotty and subtle a problem must be left to the scientist of the future to decide. Perhaps some promising young physiologist, profiting by the "George Henry Lewes Studentship" founded by George Eliot, may some day satisfactorily elucidate this question. In the meanwhile it is at least gratifying to reflect that she does not deny the future possibilities of even English and German women. She admits that conditions might arise which in their case also would be favourable to the highest creative effort; conditions which would modify the existing state of things according to which, to speak in her own scientific phraseology: "The woman of large capacity can seldom rise beyond the absorption of ideas; her physical conditions refuse to support the energy required for spontaneous activity; the voltaic pile is not strong enough to produce crystallisations."

But was the author of 'Adam Bede' not herself destined to be a triumphant refutation of her theory?

Or had those more favourable circumstances mentioned as vague possibilities already arisen in her
case ?   Not that we believe, for that matter, in the
superior claims of illustrious Frenchwomen.   It is
true George Eliot enumerates a formidable list of
names.   But on the whole we may boast of feminine
celebrities that need not shrink from the comparison.
• There is, of course, much truth in the great Eng-
lishwoman's generous praise of her French compeers.
"Mme. de Sévigné remains," she says, "the single
instance of a woman who is supreme in a class of
literature which has engaged the ambition of men ;
Mme. Dacier still reigns the queen of blue-stockings,
though women have long studied Greek without
shame ; Mme. de Staël's name still rises to the lips
when we are asked to mention a woman of great
intellectual power ; Mme. Roland is still the unrivalled type of the sagacious and sternly heroic yet
lovable woman ; George Sand is the unapproached
artist who, to Jean Jacques' eloquence and deep sense
of external nature, unites the clear delineation of
character and the tragic depth of passion."

Shall we be forced to admit that the representative
women of England cannot justly be placed on as high
a level ?   Is it so certain that they, too, did not speak
out of the fulness of their womanly natures ?   That
they too did not feel the genuine need to express
modes of thought and feeling peculiar to themselves,
which men, if at all, had but inadequately expressed
hitherto ?

Was not Queen Elizabeth the best type of a female
ruler, one whose keen penetration enabled her to
choose her ministers with infallible judgment ?   Did
not Fanny Burney distil the delicate aroma of girl-

hood in one of the most delightful of novels? Or what of Jane Austen, whose microscopic fidelity of observation has a well-nigh scientific accuracy, never equalled unless in the pages of the author we are writing of? Sir Walter Scott apparently recognised the eminently feminine inspiration of her writings, as he says: "That young lady had a talent for describing the involvements, and feelings, and characters of ordinary life, which is for me the most wonderful I ever met with. The Bow-wow strain I can do myself like any now agoing; but the exquisite touch, which renders ordinary commonplace things and characters interesting from the truth of the descriptions and the sentiment, is denied to me." Then turning to the Brontës, does not one feel the very heartbeats of womanhood in those powerful utterances that seem to spring from some central emotional energy? Again, does not Mrs. Browning occupy a unique place among poets? Is there not a distinctively womanly strain of emotion in the throbbing tides of her high-wrought melodious song? And, to come to George Eliot herself, will any one deny that, in the combination of sheer intellectual power with an unparalleled vision for the homely details of life, she takes precedence of all writers of this or any other country? To some extent this wonderful woman conforms to her own standard. She undoubtedly adds to the common fund of crystallised human experience, as literature might be called, something which is specifically feminine. But, on the other hand, her intellect excels precisely in those qualities habitually believed to be masculine, one of its chief characteristics consisting in the grasp of abstract philosophical ideas. This faculty, however, by no means impairs those instinctive processes of the imagination by which true artistic work is produced; George Eliot combining in an unusual degree the subtlest power of analysis with that happy gift of genius which enabled her to create such characters as Amos Barton, Hetty, Mrs. Poyser, Maggie, and Tom Tulliver, Godfrey Cass and Caleb Garth, which seem to come fresh from the mould of Nature itself. Indeed, she has hardly a rival among women in this power of objective imagination by which she throws her whole soul into natures of the most varied and opposite types, whereas George Sand only succeeds greatly when she is thoroughly in sympathy with her creations.

After George Eliot's eulogium of French women, one feels tempted to institute a comparison between these two great contemporaries, who occupied the same leading position in their respective countries. But it will probably always remain a question of idiosyncracy which of the two one is disposed to rank higher, George Eliot being the greatest realist, George Sand the greatest idealist, of her sex. The works of the French writer are, in fact, prose poems rather than novels. They are not studies of life, but life interpreted by the poet's vision. George Sand cannot give us a description of any scene in nature, of her own feelings, of a human character, without imparting to it some magical effect as of objects seen under the transfiguring influence of moonlight or storm clouds; whereas George Eliot loves to bathe her productions in the broad pitiless midday light, which leaves no room for illusion, but reveals all nature with uncompromising directness. The one has more of that primitive imagination which seizes on the elemental side of life—on the spectacle of the

starry heavens or of Alpine solitudes, on the insur-
rection and tumult of human passion, on the shocks
of revolution convulsing the social order—while the
other possesses, in a higher degree, the acute intel·
lectual perception for the orderly sequence of life,
for that unchangeable round of toil which is the lot
of the mass of men, and for the earth in its homelier
aspects as it tells on our daily existence. In George
Sand's finest work there is a sweet spontaneity,
almost as if she were an oracle of Nature uttering
automatically the divine message. But, on the other
hand, when the inspiration forsakes her, she drifts
along on a windy current of words, the fatal facility
of her pen often beguiling the writer into vague dif-
fuseness and unsubstantial declamation.

In this respect, also, our English novelist is the
opposite of George Sand, for George Eliot invariably
remains the master of 'her genius : indeed, she
thoroughly fulfils Goethe's demand that if you set
up for an artist you must command art. This intellectual self-restraint never forsakes George Eliot, who
always selects her means with a thorough knowledge
of the ends to be attained. The radical difference
in the genius of these two writers, to both of whom
applies Mrs. Browning's apt appellation of "large-
brained woman and large-hearted man," extends
naturally to their whole tone of thought. George
Sand is impassioned, turbulent, revolutionary, the
spiritual daughter of Rousseau, with an enthusiastic
faith in man's future destiny. George Eliot, con-
templative, observant, instinctively conservative, her
imagination dearly loving to do "a little Toryism on
the sly," is as yet the sole outcome of the modern positive spirit in imaginative literature—the sole novelist

who has incorporated in an artistic form some of the leading ideas of Comte, of Mazzini, and of Darwin. In fact, underlying all her art there is the same rigorous teaching of the inexorable laws which govern the life of man! The teaching that not liberty but duty is the condition of existence ; the teaching of the incalculable effects of hereditary transmission, with the solemn responsibilities it involves ; the teaching of the inherent sadness and imperfection in human nature, which render resignation the first virtue of man.

In fact, as a moral influence, George Eliot cannot so much be compared with George Sand, or with any other novelist of her generation, as with Carlyle. She had, indeed, a far more explicit ethical code to offer than the author of 'Sartor Resartus.' For though the immense force of the latter's personality, glowing through his writings, had a tonic effect in promoting a healthy moral tone, there was little of positive moral truth to be gathered from them. But the lessons which George Eliot would fain teach to men were most unmistakable in their bearing—the lessons of pitying love towards fellow-men ; of sympathy with all human suffering ; of unwavering faithfulness towards the social bond, consisting in the claims of race, of country, of family ; of unflagging aspiration after that life which is most beneficent to the community, that life, in short, towards which she herself aspired in the now famous prayer to reach

> " That purest heaven, be to other souls
> The cup of strength in some great agony,
> Enkindle generous ardour, feed pure love,
> Beget the smiles that have no cruelty—
> Be the sweet presence of a good diffused,
> And in diffusion ever more intense."

CHAPTER II.

CHILDHOOD AND EARLY HOME.

MARY ANN EVANS, better known as "George Eliot,"
was born on November 22nd, 1819, at South Farm,
a mile from Griff, in the parish of Colton, in Warwickshire. Both the date and place of her birth have
been incorrectly stated, hitherto, in the notices of her
life. The family moved to Griff House in March of
the following year, when she was only six months
old. Her father, Robert Evans, of Welsh origin, was
a Staffordshire man from Ellaston, near Ashbourne,
and began life as a carpenter. In the kitchen at
Griff House may still be seen a beautifully-fashioned
oaken press, a sample of his workmanship. A portrait
of him, also preserved there, is known among the
family as "Adam Bede." It is not as good a likeness as that of a certain carefully painted miniature,
the features of which bear an unmistakable resemblance to those of the daughter destined to immortalise
his name. A strongly marked, yet handsome face,
massive in structure, and with brown eyes, whose
shrewd, penetrating glance is particularly noticeable,
betoken the man of strong practical intelligence, of
rare energy and endurance. His career and character
are partially depicted in Adam Bede, Caleb Garth,
and Mr. Hackit—portraitures in which the different
stages of his life are recorded with a mingling of fact

and fiction. A shadowing forth of the same nature is discernible in the devotion of Stradivarius to his noble craft ; and even in the tender paternity of Mr. Tulliver there are indications of another phase of the same individuality.

Like Adam Bede, Mr. Evans from carpenter rose to be forester, and from forester to be land-agent. It was in the latter capacity alone that he was ever known in Warwickshire. At one time he was surveyor to five estates in the midland counties—those of Lord Aylesford, Lord Lifford, Mr. Bromley Davenport, Mrs. Gregory, and Sir Roger Newdigate. The last was his principal employer. Having early discerned the exceptional capacity of the man, Sir Roger induced him to settle in Warwickshire, and take charge of his estates. Sir Roger's seat, Arbury Hall, is the original of the charming description of Cheverel Manor in 'Mr. Gilfil's Love Story.' It is said that Mr. Evans's trustworthiness had become proverbial in the county. But while faithfully serving his employers he also enjoyed great popularity among their tenants. He was gentle, but of indomitable firmness ; and while stern to the idle and unthrifty, he did not press heavily on those who might be behindhand with their rent, owing to ill-luck or misfortune, on quarter days.

Mr. Evans was twice married. He had lost his first wife, by whom he had a son and a daughter, before settling in Warwickshire. Of his second wife, whose maiden name was Pearson, very little is known. She must, therefore, according to Schiller, have been a pattern of womanhood ; for he says that the best women, like the best ruled states, have no history. We have it on very good authority, however, that

Mrs. Hackit, in 'Amos Barton,' is a faithful likeness of George Eliot's mother. This may seem startling at first, but, on reflection, she is the woman one might have expected, being a strongly-marked figure, with a heart as tender as her tongue is sharp. She is described as a thin woman, with a chronic liver-complaint, of indefatigable industry and epigrammatic speech ; who, "in the utmost enjoyment of spoiling a friend's self-satisfaction, was never known to spoil a stocking." A notable housewife, whose clockwork regularity in all domestic affairs was such that all her farm-work was done by nine o'clock in the morning, when she would sit down to her loom. "In the same spirit, she brought out her furs on the first of November, whatever might be the temperature. She was not a woman weakly to accommodate herself to shilly-shally proceedings. If the season didn't know what it ought to do, Mrs. Hackit did. In her best days it was always sharp weather at 'Gunpowder Plot,' and she didn't like new fashions." Keenly observant and quick of temper, she was yet full of good nature, her sympathy showing itself in the active helpfulness with which she came to the assistance of poor Milly Barton, and the love she showed to her children, who, however, declined kissing her.

Is there not a strong family resemblance between this character and Mrs. Poyser, that masterpiece of George Eliot's art? Mary Ann's gift of pointed speech was therefore mother-wit, in the true sense, and her rich humour and marvellous powers of observation were derived from the same side, while her conscientiousness, her capacity, and that faculty of taking pains, which is so large a factor in the development of genius, came more directly from the father.

Mr. Evans had three children by his second wife, Christiana, Isaac, and Mary Ann. " It is interesting, I think," writes George Eliot, in reply to some questions of an American lady, " to know whether a writer was born in a central or border district—a condition which always has a strongly determining influence. I was born in Warwickshire, but certain family traditions connected with more northerly districts made these districts a region of poetry to me in my early childhood." In the autobiographical sonnets, entitled 'Brother and Sister,' we catch a glimpse of the mother preparing her children for their accustomed ramble, by stroking down the tippet and setting the frill in order ; then standing on the door-step to follow their lessening figures "with the benediction of her gaze." Mrs. Evans was aware, to a certain extent, of her daughter's unusual capacity, being anxious not only that she should have the best education attainable in the neighbourhood, but also that good moral influences should be brought to bear upon her : still, the girl's constant habit of reading, even in bed, caused the practical mother not a little annoyance.

The house, where the family lived at that time, and in which the first twenty years of Mary Ann Evans's life were spent, is situated in a rich verdant landscape, where the "grassy fields, each with a sort of personality given to it by the capricious hedge-rows," blend harmoniously with the red-roofed cottages scattered in a happy haphazard fashion amid orchards and elder-bushes. Sixty years ago the country was much more thickly wooded than now, and from the windows of Griff House might be seen the oaks and elms that had still survived from Shakespeare's forest of Arden. The house of the Evans family, half manor-house, half farm, was an old-fashioned building, two stories high, with red brick walls thickly covered with ivy. Like the Garths, they were probably "very fond of their old house." A lawn, interspersed with trees, stretched in front towards the gate, flanked by two stately Norway firs, while a sombre old yew almost touched some of the upper windows with its wide-spreading branches. A farm-yard was at the back, with low rambling sheds and stables; and beyond that, bounded by quiet meadows, one may still see the identical "leafy, flowery, bushy" garden, which George Eliot so often delighted in describing, at a time when her early life, with all its tenderly hoarded associations, had become to her but a haunting memory of bygone things. A garden where roses and cabbages jostle each other, where vegetables have to make room for gnarled old apple-trees, and where, amid the raspberry bushes and row of currant trees, you expect to come upon Hetty herself, "stooping to gather the low-hanging fruit."

Such was the place where the childhood of George Eliot was spent. Here she drew in those impressions of English rural and provincial life, of which one day she was to become the greatest interpreter. Impossible to be in a better position for seeing life. Not only was her father's position always improving, so that she was early brought in contact with different grades of society, but his calling made him more or less acquainted with all ranks of his neighbours, and, says George Eliot, "I have always thought that the most fortunate Britons are those whose experience has given them a practical share in many aspects of the national lot, who have lived long among the mixed commonalty, roughing it with them under difficulties, knowing how their food tastes to them, and getting acquainted with their notions and motives, not by inference from traditional types in literature, or from philosophical theories, but from daily fellowship and observation."

And what kind of a child was it who loitered about the farm-yard and garden and fields, noticing everything with grave, watchful eyes, and storing it in a memory of extraordinary tenacity? One of her schoolfellows, who knew her at the age of thirteen, confessed to me that it was impossible to imagine George Eliot as a baby; that it seemed as if she must have come into the world fully developed, like a second Minerva. Her features were fully formed at a very early age, and she had a seriousness of expression almost startling for her years. The records of her child-life may be deciphered, amid some romantic alterations, in the early history of Tom and Maggie Tulliver. Isaac and Mary Ann Evans were playmates, like these, the latter having all the tastes of a boy; whereas her sister Chrissy, said to be the original of Lucy Deane, had peculiarly dainty feminine ways, and shrank from out-door rambles for fear of soiling her shoes or pinafore. But Mary Ann and her brother went fishing together, or spinning tops, or digging for earth-nuts; and the twice-told incident of the little girl being left to mind the rod and losing herself in dreamy contemplation, oblivious of her task, is evidently taken from life, and may be quoted as a reminiscence of her own childhood :—

> " One day my brother left me in high charge
>   To mind the rod, while he went seeking bait,
>   And bade me, when I saw a nearing barge,
>   Snatch out the line, lest he should come too late.

Proud of the task I watched with all my might
For one whole minute, till my eyes grew wide,
Till sky and earth took on a new strange light,
And seemed a dream-world floating on some tide.

A fair pavilioned boat for me alone,
Bearing me onward through the vast unknown.

But sudden came the barge's pitch-black prow,
Nearer and angrier came my brother's cry,
And all my soul was quivering fear, when lo!
Upon the imperilled line, suspended high,

A silver perch! My guilt that won the prey
Now turned to merit, had a guerdon rich
Of hugs and praises, and made merry play
Until my triumph reached its highest pitch

When all at home were told the wondrous feat,
And how the little sister had fished well.
In secret, though my fortune tasted sweet,
I wondered why this happiness befell.

'The little lass had luck,' the gardener said;
And so I learned, luck was to glory wed."

Unlike Maggie, however, little Mary Ann was as
good a hand at fishing as her brother, only differing
from him in not liking to put the worms on the
hooks.

Another incident taken from real life, if somewnat
magnified, is the adventure with the gipsies. For the
prototype of Maggie also fell among these marauding
vagrants, and was detained a little time among them.
Whether she also proposed to instruct the gipsies and
to gain great influence over them by teaching them
something about "geography" and "Columbus," does
not transpire. But, indeed, most of Maggie's early
experiences are autobiographic, down to such facts as
her father telling her to rub her "turnip" cheeks

against Sally's to get a little bloom, and to cutting off one side of her hair in a passion. At a very early age Mary Ann and her brother were sent to the village free school at Colton, in the parish of Griff, a not unusual custom in those days, when the means of tuition for little children were much more difficult to procure than now. There are still old men living who used to sit on the same form with little Mary Ann Evans learning her A, B, C, and a certain William Jacques (the original of the delightfully comic Bob Jakins of fiction) remembers carrying her pick-a-back on the lawn in front of her father's house.

As the brother and sister grew older they saw less of each other, Mary Ann being sent to a school at Nuneaton, kept by Miss Lewis, for whom she retained an affectionate regard long years afterwards. About the same time she taught at a Sunday-school, in a little cottage adjoining her father's house. When she was twelve years old, being then, in the words of a neighbour, who occasionally called at Griff House, " a queer, three-cornered, awkward girl," who sat in corners and shyly watched her elders, she was placed as boarder with the Misses Franklin at Coventry. This school, then in high repute throughout the neighbourhood, was kept by two sisters, of whom the younger, Miss Rebecca Franklin, was a woman of unusual attainments and ladylike culture, although not without a certain taint of Johnsonian affectation. She seems to have thoroughly grounded Miss Evans in a sound English education, laying great stress in particular on the propriety of a precise and careful manner of speaking and reading. She herself always made a point of expressing herself in studied sentences, and on one occasion, when a friend had called to ask after a dying relative, she actually kept the servant waiting till she had framed an appropriately worded message. Miss Evans, in whose family a broad provincial dialect was spoken, soon acquired Miss Rebecca's carefully elaborated speech, and, not content with that, she might be said to have created a new voice for herself. In later life every one who knew her was struck by the sweetness of her voice, and the finished construction of every sentence, as it fell from her lips; for by that time the acquired habit had become second nature, and blended harmoniously with her entire personality. But in those early days the artificial effort at perfect propriety of expression was still perceptible, and produced an impression of affectation, perhaps reflecting that of her revered instructress. It is also believed that some of the beauty of her intonation in reading English poetry was owing to the same early influence.

. Mary Ann, or Marian as she came afterwards to be called, remained about three years with the Misses Franklin. She stood aloof from the other pupils, and one of her schoolfellows, Miss Bradley Jenkins, says that she was quite as remarkable in those early days as after she had acquired fame. She seems to have strangely impressed the imagination of the latter, who, figuratively speaking, looked up at her "as at a mountain." There was never anything of the school-girl about Miss Evans, for, even at that early age, she had the manners and appearance of a grave, staid woman; so much so, that a stranger, happening to call one day, mistook this girl of thirteen for one of the Misses Franklin, who were then middle-aged women. In this, also, there is a certain resemblance to Maggie Tulliver, who, at the age of thirteen, is

described as looking already like a woman. English
composition, French and German, were some of the
studies to which much time and attention were devoted. Being greatly in advance of the other pupils
in the knowledge of French, Miss Evans and Miss
Jenkins were taken out of the general class and set to
study it together ; but, though the two girls were thus
associated in a closer fellowship, no real intimacy
apparently followed from it. The latter watched the
future "George Eliot" with intense interest, but always
felt as if in the presence of a superior, though socially
their positions were much on a par. This haunting
sense of superiority precluded the growth of any closer
friendship between the two fellow-pupils. All the
more startling was it to the admiring schoolgirl, when
one day, on using Marian Evans's German dictionary,
she saw scribbled on its blank page some verses,
evidently original, expressing rather sentimentally a
yearning for love and sympathy. Under this granite-
like exterior, then, there was beating a heart that
passionately craved for human tenderness and companionship!

Inner solitude was no doubt the portion of George
Eliot in those days. She must already have had a dim
consciousness of unusual power, to a great extent isolating her from the girls of her own age, absorbed as
they were in quite other feelings and ideas. Strong
religious convictions pervaded her life at this period,
and in the fervid faith and spiritual exaltation which
characterise Maggie's girlhood, we have a very faithful
picture of the future novelist's own state of mind.
Passing through many stages of religious thought,
she was first simple Church of England, then Low
Church, then "Anti-Supernatural." In this latter

character she wore an "Anti-Supernatural" cap, in which, so says an early friend, "her plain features looked all the plainer." But her nature was a mixed one, as indeed is Maggie's too, and conflicting tendencies and inclinations pulled her, no doubt, in different directions. The self-renouncing impulses of one moment were checkmated at another by an eager desire for approbation and distinguishing pre-eminence; and a piety verging on asceticism did not exclude, on the other hand, a very clear perception of the advantages and desirability of good birth, wealth, and high social position. Like her own charming Esther in 'Felix Holt,' she had a fine sense, amid somewhat anomalous surroundings, of the highest refinements and delicacies which are supposed to be the natural attributes of people of rank and fashion. She even shared with the above-mentioned heroine certain girlish vanities and weaknesses, such as liking to have all things about her person as elegant as possible.

About the age of fifteen Marian Evans left the Misses Franklin, and soon afterwards she had the misfortune of losing her mother, who died in her forty-ninth year. Writing to a friend in after life she says, "I began at sixteen to be acquainted with the unspeakable grief of a last parting, in the death of my mother." Less sorrowful partings ensued, though in the end they proved almost as irrevocable., Her elder sister, and the brother in whose steps she had once followed "puppy-like," married and settled in homes of their own. Their different lots in life, and the far more pronounced differences of their aims and ideas, afterwards divided the "brother and sister" completely This kind of separation between people who have been friends in youth is often more terrible to endure

than the actual loss by death itself, and doth truly
" work like madness in the brain." Is there not some
reference to this in that pathetic passage in 'Adam
Bede:' "Family likeness has often a deep sadness
in it. Nature, that great tragic dramatist, knits us
together by bone and muscle, and divides us by the
subtler web of our brains, blends yearning and repulsion, and ties us by our heartstrings to the beings that
jar us at every movement .... we see eyes—ah! so
like our mother's, averted from us in cold alienation."

For some years after this Miss Evans and her
father remained alone together at Griff House. He
offered to get a housekeeper, as not the house
only, but farm matters, had to be looked after, and
he was always tenderly considerate of "the little
wench" as he called her. But his daughter preferred
taking the whole management of the place into her
own hands, and she was as conscientious and diligent
in the discharge of her domestic duties as in the prosecution of the studies she carried on at the same
time. One of her chief beauties was in her large, finely-
shaped, feminine hands—hands which she has, indeed,
described as characteristic of several of her heroines ;
but she once pointed out to a friend at Foleshill that
one of them was broader across than the other, saying,
with some pride, that it was due to the quantity of
butter and cheese she had made during her house-
keeping days at Griff. It will be remembered that
this is a characteristic attributed to the exemplary
Nancy Lammeter, whose person gave one the idea of
" perfect unvarying neatness as the body of a little
bird," only her hands bearing "the traces of butter
making, cheese crushing, and even still coarser work."
Certainly the description of the dairy in 'Adam Bede,'

and all the processes of butter making, is one which only complete knowledge could have rendered so perfect. Perhaps no scene in all her novels stands out with more life-like vividness than that dairy which one could have sickened for in hot, dusty streets: "Such coolness, such purity, such fresh fragrance of new-pressed cheese, of firm butter, of wooden vessels perpetually bathed in pure water; such soft colouring of red earthenware and creamy surfaces, brown wood and polished tin, grey limestone and rich orange-red rust on the iron weights and hooks and hinges."

This life of mixed practical activity and intellectual pursuits came to an end in 1841, when Mr. Evans relinquished Griff House, and the management of Sir Roger Newdigate's estates, to his married son, and removed with his daughter to Foleshill, near Coventry.

CHAPTER III.

YOUTHFUL STUDIES AND FRIENDSHIPS.

THE period from about twenty to thirty is usually the most momentous in the lives of illustrious men and women. It is true that the most abiding impressions, those which the future author will reproduce most vividly, have been absorbed by the growing brain previous to this age; but the fusion of these varied impressions of the outward world with the inner life, and the endless combinations in which imagination delights, rarely begin before. Then, as a rule, the ideas are engendered to be carried out in the maturity of life. Alfred de Vigny says truly enough:

" Qu'est-ce qu'une grande vie ?
Une pensée de la jeunesse, exécutée par l'âge mur."

Moreover, it is a revolutionary age. Inherited opinions that had been accepted, as the rotation of the seasons, with unhesitating acquiescence, become an object of speculation and passionate questioning. Nothing is taken upon trust. The intellect, stimulated by the sense of expanding and hitherto unchecked capacity, delights in exercising its strength by critically passing in review the opinions, laws, institutions commonly accepted as unalterable. And if the intellect is thus active the heart is still more so,

This is emphatically the time of enthusiastic friend-ship and glowing love, if often also of cruel dis-enchantment and disillusion. In most biographies, therefore, this phase of life is no less fascinating than instructive. For it shows the individual while still in a stage of growth already reacting on his environment, and becoming a motive power according to the measure of his intellectual and moral endow-ments.

It is on this state of George Eliot's life that we are now entering. At Foleshill she acquired that vast range of knowledge and universality of culture which so eminently distinguished her.

The house she now inhabited though not nearly as picturesque or substantial as the former home of the Evanses, was yet sufficiently spacious, with a pleasant garden in front and behind it; the latter, Marian Evans was fond of making as much like the deli-cious garden of her childhood as was possible under the circumstances. In other respects she greatly altered her ways of life, cultivating an ultra-fastidious-ness in her manners and household arrangements. Though so young she was not only entire mistress of her father's establishment but, as his business required him to be abroad the greater pa' 'f each week, she was mostly alone.

Her life now became more and more that of a student, one of her chief reasons for rejoicing at the change of residence being the freer access to books. She had, however, already amassed quite a library of her own by this time. In addition to her private studies, she was now also able to have masters to instruct her in a variety of subjects. The Rev. T. Sheepshanks, head-master of the Coventry Grammar-school, gave her

lessons in Greek and Latin, as she particularly wished
to learn the former language in order to read
Æschylus.   She continued her study of French,
German, and Italian under the tuition of Signor
Brezzi, even acquiring some knowledge of Hebrew
by her own unassisted efforts. Mr. Simms, the veteran
organist of St. Michael's, Coventry, instructed her
in the pianoforte ; and probably Rosamond Vincy's
teacher in 'Middlemarch' is a faithful portraiture of
him.   " Her master at Mrs. Lemon's school (close to
a country town with a memorable history that had its
relics in church and castle) was one of those excellent
musicians here and there to be found in the provinces,
worthy to compare with many a noted Kapellmeister
in a country which offers more plentiful conditions
of musical celebrity."   George Eliot's sympathetic
rendering of her favourite composers, particularly
Beethoven and Schubert, was always delightful to her
friends, although connoisseurs considered her possessed of little or no strictly technical knowledge.
Be that as it may, many an exquisite passage scattered up and down her works, bears witness to her
heartfelt appreciation of music, which seems to have
had a more intimate attraction for her than the fine
arts.   She shows little feeling for archæological
beauties, in which Warwickshire is so rich : in her
' Scenes of Clerical Life' dismissing a fine monument
of Lady Jane Grey, a genuine specimen of old Gothic
art at Astley Church, with a sneer about "marble
warriors, and their wives without noses."

In spite of excessive study, this period of Marian's
life is not without faint echoes of an early love-story
of her own.   In the house of one of her married half-
sisters she met a young man who promised, at that

time, to take a distinguished position in his profession. A kind of engagement, or semi-engagement, took place, which Mr. Evans refused to countenance, and finally his daughter broke it off in a letter, showing both her strong sense and profoundly affectionate nature. At this time she must have often had a painful consciousness of being cut off from that living fellowship with the like-minded so stimulating to the intellectual life. Men are not so subject to this form of soul hunger as women; for at their public schools and colleges they are brought into contact with their contemporaries, and cannot fail to find comrades amongst them of like thoughts and aspirations with themselves. A fresh life, however, at once vivifying to her intellect and stimulating to her heart, now began for Marian Evans in the friendship she formed with Mr. and Mrs. Charles Bray of Rosehill, Coventry. Rahel—the subtly gifted German woman, whose letters and memoirs are a treasury of delicate observation and sentiment— observes that people of marked spiritual affinities are bound to meet some time or other in their lives. If not entirely true, there is a good deal to be said for this comforting theory ; as human beings of similar nature seem constantly converging as by some magnetic attraction.

The circle to which Miss Evans now happened to be introduced was in every sense congenial and inspiriting. Mr. Bray, his wife, and his sister-in-law were a trio more like some delightful characters in a first-rate novel than the sober inhabitants of a Warwickshire country town. Living in a house beautifully situated on the outskirts of Coventry, they used to spend their lives in philosophical speculations, philanthropy, and pleasant social hospitality, joining to the ease and *laisser aller* of continental manners a thoroughly English geniality and trust-worthiness.

Mr. Bray was a wealthy ribbon manufacturer, but had become engrossed from an early age in religious and metaphysical speculation as well as in political and social questions. Beginning to inquire into the dogmas which formed the basis of his belief, he found, on careful investigation, that they did not stand, in his opinion, the test of reason. His arguments set his brother-in-law, Mr. Charles C. Hennell, a Unitarian, to examine afresh and go carefully over the whole ground of popular theology, the consequence of this close study being the 'Inquiry concerning the Origin of Christianity,' a work which attracted a good deal of attention when it appeared, and was translated into German at the instance of David Strauss. It was published in 1838, a few years after the appearance of the 'Life of Jesus.' In its critical examination of the miracles, and in the sifting of mythological from historical elements in the Gospels it bears considerable analogy to Strauss's great work, although strictly based on inde-pendent studies, being originally nothing more than an attempt to solve the doubts of a small set of friends. Their doubts were solved, but not in the manner originally anticipated.

Mrs. Bray, of an essentially religious nature, shared the opinions of her husband and brother, and without conforming to the external rites and ceremonies of a creed, led a life of saintly purity and self-devotion. The exquisite beauty of her moral nature not only attracted Marian to this truly amiable woman, but filled her with reverence, and the friend-ship then commenced was only ended by death.

In Miss Sara Hennell, Marian Evans found another congenial companion who became as a sister to her. This singular being, in most respects such a contrast to her sister, high-strung, nervous, excitable, importing all the ardour of feeling into a life of austere thought, seemed in a manner mentally to totter under the weight of her own immense metaphysical specula-tions. A casual acquaintance of these two young ladies might perhaps have predicted that Miss Hennell was the one destined to achieve fame in the future, and she certainly must have been an extraordinary mental stimulus to her young friend Marian. These gifted sisters, two of a family, all the members of which were remarkable, by some are identified as the originals of the de-lightful Meyrick household in 'Daniel Deronda.' Each member of this genial group was already, or ultimately became, an author of more or less repute. A reviewer in the 'Westminster,' writing of Mr. Bray's philosophical publications, some years ago, said: "If he would reduce his many works to one containing nothing unessential, he would doubtless obtain that high place among the philosophers of our country to which his powers of thought entitle him." His most popular book, called 'The Education of the Feelings,' intended for use in secular schools, deals with the laws of morality practically applied. Mrs. Bray's writings, on the same order of subjects, are still further simplified for the understanding of children. She is the authoress of 'Physiology for Schools,' 'The British Empire,' 'Elements of Mo-rality,' etc. Her 'Duty to Animals' has become a class book in the schools of the midland counties, and she was one of the first among those noble-hearted men and women who have endeavoured to introduce a greater degree of humanity into our treatment of animals.

George Eliot, writing to Mrs. Bray in March 1873 on this very subject, says :

"A very good, as well as very rich, woman, Mrs. S—, has founded a model school at Naples, and has the sympathy of the best Italians in her educational efforts. Of course a chief point in trying to improve the Italians is to teach them kindness to animals, and a friend of Mrs. S— has confided to her a small sum of money—fifty pounds, I think—to be applied to the translation and publication of some good books for young people, which would be likely to rouse in them a sympathy with dumb creatures.

" Will you kindly help me in the effort to further Mrs. S—'s good work by sending me a copy of your book on animals, and also by telling me the periodical in which the parts of the book first appeared, as well as the titles of any other works which you think would be worth mentioning for the purpose in question ?

" Mrs. S— (as indeed you may probably know) is the widow of a German merchant of Manchester, as rich as many such merchants are, and as benevolent as only the choicest few. She knows all sorts of good work for the world, and is known by most of the workers. It struck me, while she was speaking of this need of a book to translate, that you had done the very thing."

A few days later the following highly interesting letter came from the same source :

"Many thanks for the helpful things you have sent

me. 'The Wounded Bird' is charming. But now something very much larger of the same kind must be written, and you are the person to write it—something that will bring the emotions, sufferings, and possible consolations of the dear brutes vividly home to the imaginations of children : fitted for children of all countries, as Reineke Fuchs is comprehensible to all nations. A rough notion came to me the other day of supposing a house of refuge, not only for dogs, but for all distressed animals. The keeper of this refuge understands the language of the brutes, which includes differences of dialect not hindering communication even between birds and dogs, by the help of some Ulysses among them who is versed in the various tongues, and puts in the needed explanations. Said keeper overhears his refugees solacing their evenings by telling the story of their experiences, and finally acts as editor of their autobiographies. I imagine my long-loved fellow-creature, the ugly dog, telling the sorrows and the tender emotions of gratitude which have wrought him into a sensitive soul. The donkey is another cosmopolitan sufferer, and a greater martyr than Saint Lawrence. If we only knew what fine motives he has for his meek endurance, and how he loves a friend who will scratch his nose !

"All this is not worth anything except to make you feel how much better a plan you can think of.

"Only you must positively write this book which everybody wants—this book which will do justice to the share our 'worthy fellow-labourers' have had in the groaning and travailing of the world towards the birth of the right and fair.

"But you must not do it without the 'sustenance

of labour '—I don't say 'pay,' since there is no pay for good work. Let Mr. . . . be blest with the blessing of the unscrupulous. I want to contribute something towards helping the brutes, and helping the children, especially the southern children, to be good to the creatures who are continually at their mercy. I can't write the needed book myself, but I feel sure that you can, and that you will not refuse the duty."

Mrs. Bray's answer to this humorous suggestion may be gathered from George Eliot's amiable reply :

"I see at once that you must be right about the necessity for being simple and literal. In fact I have ridiculous impulses in teaching children, and always make the horizon too wide.

"'The Wounded Bird' is perfect of its kind, and that kind is the best for a larger work. You yourself see clearly that it is an exceptional case for any one to be able to write books for children without putting in them false morality disguised as devout religion. And you are one of the exceptional cases. I am quite sure, from what you have done, that you can do the thing which is still wanted to be done. As to imagination, 'The Wounded Bird' is full of imagination."

These extracts pleasantly illustrate both the writer and recipient of such humane letters ; and, though written at a much later period, not only give an idea of the nature of Mrs. Bray's literary pursuits, but of the friendly relations subsisting to the end between her and George Eliot.

Of Miss Hennell's work it is more difficult to speak without entering more deeply into her subject-matter than is compatible with the scope of the present work.

YOUTHFUL STUDIES AND FRIENDSHIPS. 31

In one of her best known books, entitled 'Thoughts
in Aid of Faith,' she makes the daring attempt to
trace the evolution of religion, her mode of thought
partaking at once of the scientific and the mystical.
For the present she seems to be one of the very
few women who have ventured into the arena of
philosophy; and, curiously enough, her doctrine is
that there should be a feminine method in metaphysics as well as a masculine, the sexes, according
to this singular theory, finding their counterpart in
religion and science. It may be remembered that
George Eliot, in one of her essays, is of opinion that
women should endeavour to make some distinctively
feminine contributions to the intellectual pursuits they
engage in, saying, "Let the whole field of reality be
laid open to woman as well as to man, and then that
which is peculiar in her mental modification, instead
of being, as it is now, a source of discord and repulsion
between the sexes, will be found to be a necessary
complement to the truth and beauty of life. Then
we shall have that marriage of minds which alone can
blend all the hues of thought and feeling in one lovely
rainbow of promise for the harvest of happiness."
Something of the same idea lies at the root of much
in Miss Hennell's mystical disquisitions.

This circumstantial account of the circle to which
Miss Evans was now introduced has been given, because
it consisted of friends who, more than any others,
helped in the growth and formation of her mind. No
human being, indeed, can be fully understood without
some knowledge of the companions that at one time or
other, but especially during the period of development,
have been intimately associated with his or her life.
However vastly a mountain may appear to loom

above us from the plain, on ascending to its summit
one always finds innumerable lesser eminences which
all help in making up the one imposing central
effect. And similarly in the world of mind, many
superior natures, in varying degrees, all contribute
their share towards the maturing of that exceptional
intellectual product whose topmost summit is genius.

The lady who first introduced Marian Evans to the
Brays was not without an object of her own, for her
young friend—whose religious fervour, tinged with
evangelical sentiment, was as conspicuous as her
unusual learning and thoughtfulness—seemed to her
peculiarly fitted to exercise a beneficial influence on
the Rosehill household, where generally unorthodox
opinions were much in vogue.

Up to the age of seventeen or eighteen Marian had
been considered the most truly pious member of her
family, being earnestly bent, as she says, "to shape
this anomalous English Christian life of ours into some
consistency with the spirit and simple verbal tenor of
the New Testament." "I was brought up," she informs
another correspondent, "in the Church of England,
and have never joined any other religious society ; but
I have had close acquaintance with many dissenters
of various sects, from Calvinistic Anabaptists to Uni-
tarians." Her inner life at this time is faithfully
mirrored in the spiritual experiences of Maggie Tulliver. Marian Evans was not one who could rest satisfied with outward observances and lip-worship : she
needed a faith which should give unity and sanctity to
the conception of life; which should awaken "that
recognition of something to be lived for beyond the
mere satisfaction of self, which is to the moral life
what the addition of a great central ganglion is to

animal life." At one time Evangelicalism supplied her with the most essential conditions of a religious life : with all the vehemence of an ardent nature she flung her whole soul into a passionate acceptance of the teaching of Christianity, carrying her zeal to the pitch of asceticism.

This was the state of her mind, at the age of seventeen, when her aunt from Wirksworth came to stay with her. Mrs. Elizabeth Evans (who came afterwards to be largely identified with Dinah Morris) was a zealous Wesleyan, having at one time been a noted preacher ; but her niece, then a rigid Calvinist, hardly thought her doctrine strict enough. When this same aunt paid her a visit, some years afterwards, at Foleshill, Marian's views had already undergone a complete transformation, and their intercourse was constrained and painful ; for the young evangelical enthusiast, who had been a favourite in clerical circles, was now, in what she afterwards described as a "crude state of freethinking." It was a period of transition through which she gradually passed into a new religious synthesis.

Her intimacy with the Brays began about the time when these new doubts were beginning to ferment in her. Her expanding mind, nourished on the best literature, ancient and modern, began to feel cramped by dogmas that had now lost their vitality ; yet a break with an inherited form of belief to which a thousand tender associations bound her, was a catastrophe she shrank from with dread. Hence a period of mental uncertainty and trouble. In consequence of these inward questionings, it happened that the young lady who had been unwittingly brought to convert her new acquaintances was converted by them. In inter-

D

course with them she was able freely to open her mind, their enlightened views helping her in this crisis of her spiritual life ; and she found it an intense relief to feel no longer bound to reconcile her moral and intellectual perceptions with a particular form of worship.

The antagonism she met with in certain quarters, the social persecution from which she had much to suffer, are perhaps responsible for some of the sharp, caustic irony with which she afterwards assailed certain theological habits of thought. It is not unlikely that in some of her essays for the *Westminster Review* she mainly expressed the thoughts which were stirred in her by the opposition she encountered at this period of her life—as, for example, in the brilliant paper entitled 'Worldliness and Otherworldliness,' which contains such a scathing passage as the following :

"For certain other elements of virtue, which are of more obvious importance to untheological minds,—a delicate sense of our neighbour's rights, an active participation in the joys and sorrows of our fellow-men, a magnanimous acceptance of privation or suffering for ourselves when it is the condition of good to others, in a word, the extension and intensification of our sympathetic nature, we think it of some importance to contend, that they have no more direct relation to the belief in a future state than the interchange of gases in the lungs has to the plurality of worlds. Nay, to us it is conceivable that to some minds the deep pathos lying in the thought of human mortality—that we are here for a little while and then vanish away, that this earthly life is all that is given to our loved ones, and to our many suffering fellow-men, lies nearer the fountains of moral emotion than the conception of extended existence. . . . To us it is matter of unmixed rejoicing that this latter necessity of healthful life is independent of theological ink, and that its evolution is ensured in the interaction of human souls as certainly as the evolution of science or of art, with which, indeed, it is but a twin ray, melting into them with undefinable limits."

It was, of course, inevitable that her changed tone of mind should attract the attention of the family and friends of Marian, and that the backsliding of so exemplary a member should afford matter for scandal in many a clerical circle and evangelical tea-meeting. Close to the Evanses there lived at that time a dissenting minister, whose daughter Mary was a particular favourite of Marian Evans. There had been much neighbourly intimacy between the two young ladies, and though there was only five years' difference between them, Marian always inspired her friend with a feeling of awe at her intellectual superiority. · Yet her sympathy—that sympathy with all human life which was the strongest element of her character—was even then so irresistible that every little trouble of Mary's life was entrusted to her keeping. But the sudden discovery of their daughter's friend being an "infidel" came with the shock of a thunderclap on the parents. Much hot argument passed between the minister and this youthful controversialist, but the former clinched the whole question by a triumphant reference to the dispersion of the Jews throughout the world as an irrefutable proof of the divine inspiration of the Bible. In spite of this vital difference on religious questions, Miss Evans was suffered to go on giving the minister's daughter lessons in German, which were continued for two or three

years, she having generously undertaken this labour
of love twice a week, because she judged from the
shape of her young friend's head—phrenology being
rife in those days—that she must have an excellent
understanding. But, better than languages, she taught
her the value of time, always cutting short mere
random talk by simply ignoring it. Altogether the
wonderful strength of her personality manifested itself
even at this early period in the indelible impression
it left on her pupil's memory, many of her sayings
remaining graven on it as on stone. As, for instance,
when one day twitting Mary's too great self-esteem she
remarked, "We are very apt to measure ourselves by
our aspiration instead of our performance." Or when
on a friend's asking, "What is the meaning of Faust?"
she replied, "The same as the meaning of the universe." While reading '*Wallenstein's Lager*,' with her
young pupil, the latter happened to say how life-like
the characters seemed : "Don't say *seemed*," exclaimed
Marian ; "we know that they *are* true to the life."
And she immediately began repeating the talk of
labourers, farriers, butchers, and others of that class,
with such close imitation as to startle her friend. Is
not this a fore-shadowing of the inimitable scene at
the 'Rainbow?'

By far the most trying consequence of her change
of views was that now, for the first time, Marian was
brought into collision with her father, whose pet she
had always been. He could not understand her
inward perplexities, nor the need of her soul for
complete inward unity of thought, a condition impossible to her under the limiting conditions of a
dogmatic evangelicalism, "where folly often mistakes
itself for wisdom, ignorance gives itself airs of know-

ledge, and selfishness, turning its eyes upwards, calls itself religion." She, on the other hand, after a painful struggle, wanted to break away from the old forms of worship, and refused to go to church. Deeply attached though she was to her father, the need to make her acts conform with her convictions became irresistible. Under such conflicting tendencies a rupture between father and daughter became imminent, and for a short time a breaking up of the home was contemplated, Marian intending to go and live by herself in Coventry. One of the leading traits in her nature was its adhesiveness, however, and the threat of separation proved so painful to her that her friends, Mr. and Mrs. Bray, persuaded her to conform to her father's wishes as far as outward observances were implied, and for the rest he did not trouble himself to inquire into her thoughts or occupations.

From a letter written at this period it appears that the 'Inquiry Concerning the Origin of Christianity' had made a most powerful impression on her mind. Indeed, she dated from it a new birth. But so earnest and conscientious was she in her studies, that before beginning its longed-for perusal, she and a friend determined to read the Bible through again from beginning to end.

The intimacy between the inmates of Rosehill and the girl student at Foleshill meanwhile was constantly growing closer. They met daily, and in their midst the humorous side of her nature expanded no less than her intellect. Although striking ordinary acquaintances by an abnormal gravity, when completely at her ease she at times bubbled over with fun and gaiety, irradiated by the unexpected flashes of a wit whose full scope was probably as yet unsuspected by its possessor. Not but that Miss Evans and her friends must have been conscious, even at that early age, of extraordinary powers in her, destined some day to give her a conspicuous position in the world. For her conversation was already so full of charm, depth, and comprehensiveness, that all talk after hers seemed stale and common-place. Many were the discussions in those days between Mr. Bray and Marian Evans, and though frequently broken off in fierce dispute one evening, they always began again quite amicably the next. Mr. Bray probably exercised considerable influence on his young friend's mind at this impressible period of life ; perhaps her attention to philosophy was first roused by acquaintance with him, and his varied acquirements in this department may have helped in giving a positive direction to her own thoughts.

Mr. Bray was just then working out his 'Philosophy of Necessity,' the problems discussed being the same as those which have occupied the leading thinkers of the day : Auguste Comte in his ' Positive Philosophy ;' Buckle in his 'History of Civilization ;' and Mr. Herbert Spencer in his ' Sociology.' The theory that, as an individual and collectively, man is as much subject to law as any of the other entities in nature, was one of those magnificent ideas which revolutionise the world of thought. Many minds, in different countries, of different calibre, were all trying to systematise what knowledge there was on this subject in order to convert hypothesis into demonstration. To what extent Mr. Bray may have based his 'Philosophy of Necessity' on independent research, or how much was merely assimilated from contemporary sources, we cannot here inquire. Enough that the ideas embodied in it represented some of the most vital thought of the age, and contributed therefore not a little to the formation of George Eliot's mind, and to the grip which she presently displayed in the handling of philosophical topics.

In 1842 the sensation created by Dr. Strauss's *Leben Jesu* had even extended to so remote a district as Warwickshire. Some persons of advanced opinions, deeply impressed by its penetrating historical criticism, which was in fact Niebuhr's method applied to the elucidation of the Gospels, were very desirous of obtaining an English translation of this work ; meeting at the house of a common friend, the late Mr. Joseph Parkes of Birmingham, they agreed, in the first blush of their enthusiasm, to raise amongst them whatever sum might be required for the purpose. Mr. Hennell, the leading spirit in this enterprise, proposed that the translation should be undertaken by Miss Brabant, the accomplished daughter of Dr. Brabant, a scholar deeply versed in theological matters, who was in friendly correspondence with Strauss and Paulus in Germany and with Coleridge and Grote in England. The lady in question, though still in her teens, was peculiarly fitted for the task, as she had already translated some of Baur's erudite writings on theological subjects into English. But when she had done about one half of the first volume, her learned labours came to an unexpected conclusion, as she became engaged to Mr. Hennell, who to great mental attainments joined much winning buoyancy of manner. And on her marriage with this gentleman she had to relinquish her task as too laborious.

Miss Brabant's acquaintance with Marian began in

1843, and in the summer of that year the whole friendly group started on an excursion to Tenby. During their stay at this watering-place the lady who had begun, and the lady destined eventually to accomplish, the enormous labour of translating the 'Life of Jesus' gave tokens of feminine frivolity by insisting on going to a public ball, where, however, they were disappointed, as partners were very scarce. It should be remembered that Marian Evans was only twenty-three years old at this time, but, though she had not yet done anything, her friends already thought her a wonderful woman. She never seems to have had any real youthfulness, and her personal appearance greatly improved with time. It is only to the finest natures, it should be remembered, that age gives an added beauty and distinction; for the most persistent self has then worked its way to the surface, having modified the expression, and to some extent the features, to its own likeness.

There exists a coloured sketch done by Mrs. Bray about this period, which gives one a glimpse of George Eliot in her girlhood. In those Foleshill days she had a quantity of soft pale-brown hair worn in ringlets. Her head was massive, her features powerful and rugged, her mouth large but shapely, the jaw singularly square for a woman, yet having a certain delicacy of outline. A neutral tone of colouring did not help to relieve this general heaviness of structure, the complexion being pale but not fair. Nevertheless the play of expression and the wonderful mobility of the mouth, which increased with age, gave a womanly softness to the countenance in curious contrast with its framework. Her eyes, of a grey-blue, constantly varying in colour, striking some as intensely blue, others as of a pale, washed-out grey, were small and not beautiful in themselves, but when she grew animated in conversation, those eyes lit up the whole face, seeming in a manner to transfigure it. So much was this the case, that a young lady, who had once enjoyed an hour's conversation with her, came away under its spell with the impression that she was beautiful, but afterwards, on seeing George Eliot again when she was not talking, she could hardly believe her to be the same person. The charm of her nature disclosed itself in her manner and in her voice, the latter recalling that of Dorothea, in being "like the voice of a soul that has once lived in an Æolian harp." It was low and deep, vibrating with sympathy.

Mr. Bray, an enthusiastic believer in phrenology, was so much struck with the grand proportions of her head that he took Marian Evans to London to have a cast taken. He thinks that, after that of Napoleon, her head showed the largest development from brow to ear of any person's recorded. The similarity of type between George Eliot's face and Savonarola's has been frequently pointed out. Some affinity in their natures may have led her, if unconsciously, to select that epoch of Florentine life in which he played so prominent a part.

Though not above the middle height Marian gave people the impression of being much taller than she really was, her figure, although thin and slight, being well-poised and not without a certain sturdiness of make. She was never robust in health, being delicately strung, and of a highly nervous temperament. In youth the keen excitability of her nature often made her wayward and hysterical. In fact her extra-

ordinary intellectual vigour did not exclude the susceptibilities and weaknesses of a peculiarly feminine
organisation. With all her mental activity she yet
led an intensely emotional life, a life which must have
held hidden trials for her, as in those days she was
known by her friends "to weep bucketfuls of tears."

A woman of strong passions, like her own Maggie,
deeply affectionate by nature, of a clinging tenderness
of disposition, Marian Evans went through much
inward struggle, through many painful experiences
before she reached the moral self-government of her
later years. Had she not, it is hardly likely that
she could have entered with so deep a comprehension into the most intricate windings of the human
heart. That, of course, was to a great extent
due to her sympathy, sympathy being the strongest
quality of her moral nature. She flung herself,
as it were, into other lives, making their affairs,
their hopes, their sorrows her own. And this power
of identifying herself with the people she came
near had the effect of a magnet in attracting her
fellow-creatures. If friends went to her in their
trouble they would find not only that she entered with
deep feeling into their most minute concerns, but that,
by gradual degrees, she lifted them beyond their personal distress, and that they would leave her presence
in an ennobled and elevated frame of mind. This
sympathy was closely connected with her faculty of
detecting and responding to anything that showed the
smallest sign of intellectual vitality. She essentially
resembled Socrates in her manner of eliciting whatso-
ever capacity for thought might be latent in the people
she came in contact with : were it only a shoemaker
or day-labourer, she would never rest till she had

found out in what points that particular man differed from other men of his class. She always rather educed what was in others than impressed herself on them ; showing much kindliness of heart in drawing out people who were shy. Sympathy was the key-note of her nature, the source of her iridescent humour, of her subtle knowledge of character, and of her dramatic genius.

CHAPTER IV.

TRANSLATION OF STRAUSS AND FEUERBACH.— TOUR ON THE CONTINENT.

MISS BRABANT'S marriage to Mr. Charles Hennell occurred some months after this excursion to Tenby. In the meanwhile it was settled that Miss Evans should continue her translation of Dr. Strauss's *Leben Jesu.* Thus her first introduction to literature was in a sense accidental. The result proved her admirably fitted for the task; for her version of this searching and voluminous work remains a masterpiece of clear nervous English, at the same time faithfully rendering the spirit of the original. But it was a vast and laborious undertaking, requiring a large share of patience, will, and energy, quite apart from the necessary mental qualifications. On this occasion, to fit herself more fully for her weighty task, Marian taught herself a considerable amount of Hebrew. But she groaned, at times, under the pressure of the toil which had necessarily to be endured, feeling tempted to relinquish what must often have seemed almost intolerable drudgery. The active interest and encouragement of her friends, however, tided her over these moments of discouragement, and after three years of assiduous application, the translation was finally completed, and brought out by Dr.

(then Mr.) John Chapman in 1846. It is probably safe to assume that the composition of none of her novels cost George Eliot half the effort and toil which this translation had done. Yet so badly is this kind of literary work remunerated, that twenty pounds was the sum paid for what had cost three years of hard labour!

Indeed, by this time, most of the twelve friends who had originally guaranteed the sum necessary for the translation and publication of the 'Life of Jesus,' had conveniently forgotten the matter; and had it not been for the generosity of Mr. Joseph Parkes, who volunteered to advance the necessary funds, who knows how long the MS. translation might have lain dormant in a drawer at Foleshill? It no sooner saw the light, however, than every one recognised the exceptional merits of the work. And for several years afterwards Miss Evans continued to be chiefly known as the translator of Strauss's *Leben Jesu.*

Soon after relieving Miss Brabant from the task of translation, Miss Evans went to stay for a time with her friend's father, Dr. Brabant, who sadly felt the loss of his daughter's intelligent and enlivening companionship. No doubt the society of this accomplished scholar, described by Mr. Grote as "a vigorous self-thinking intellect," was no less congenial than instructive to his young companion; while her singular mental acuteness and affectionate womanly ways were most grateful to the lonely old man. There is something very attractive in this episode of George Eliot's life. It recalls a frequently recurring situation in her novels, particularly that touching one of the self-renouncing devotion with which the ardent Romola throws herself into her afflicted father's learned and recondite pursuits.

There exists a letter written to an intimate friend in 1846, soon after the translation of Strauss was finished, which, I should say, already shows the future novelist in embryo. In this delightfully humorous mystification of her friends, Miss Evans pretends that, to her gratification, she has actually had a visit from a real live German professor, whose musty person was encased in a still mustier coat. This learned personage has come over to England with the single purpose of getting his voluminous writings translated into English. There are at least twenty volumes, all unpublished, owing to the envious machinations of rival authors, none of them treating of anything more modern than Cheops, or the invention of the hieroglyphics. The respectable professor's object in coming to England is to secure a wife and translator in one. But though, on inquiry, he finds that the ladies engaged in translation are legion, they mostly turn out to be utterly incompetent, besides not answering to his requirements in other respects; the qualifications he looks for in a wife, besides a thorough acquaintance with English and German, being personal ugliness and a snug little capital, sufficient to supply him with a moderate allowance of tobacco and *Schwarzbier*, after defraying the expense of printing his books. To find this phœnix among women he is sent to Coventry on all hands.

In Miss Evans, so she runs on, the aspiring professor finds his utmost wishes realised, and so proposes to her on the spot; thinking that it may be her last chance, she accepts him with equal celerity, and her father, although strongly objecting to a foreigner, is induced to give his consent for the same reason. The lady's only stipulation is that her future husband shall take her out of England, with its dreary climate and drearier inhabitants. This being settled, she invites her friends to come to her wedding, which is to take place next week.

This lively little *jeu d'esprit* is written in the wittiest manner, and one cannot help fancying that this German Dryasdust contained the germ of one of her very subtlest masterpieces in characterisation, that of the much-to-be-pitied Casaubon, the very Sysiphus of authors. In the lady, too, willing to marry her parchment-bound suitor for the sake of co-operating in his abstruse mental labours, we have a faint adumbration of the simple-minded Dorothea.

But these sudden stirrings at original invention did not prevent Miss Evans from undertaking another task, similar to her last, if not so laborious. She now set about translating Ludwig Feuerbach's *Wesen des Christenthums.* This daring philosopher, who kept aloof from professional honours, and dwelt apart in a wood, that he might be free to handle questions of theology and metaphysics with absolute fearlessness, had created a great sensation by his philosophical criticism in Germany. Unlike his countrymen, whose writings on these subjects are usually enveloped in such an impenetrable mist that their most perilous ideas pass harmlessly over the heads of the multitude, Feuerbach, by his keen incisiveness of language and luminousness of exposition, was calculated to bring his meaning home to the average reader. Mr. Garnett's account of the 'Essence of Christianity' in the 'Encyclopædia Britannica,' admirably concise as it is, may be quoted here, as conveying in the fewest words the gist of this " famous treatise, where Feuerbach shows that every article of Christian belief corresponds to some instinct or necessity of man's nature, from which he infers that it is the creation and embodiment of some human wish, hope, or apprehension. . . . Following up the hint of one of the oldest Greek philosophers, he demonstrates that religious ideas have their counterparts in human nature, and assumes that they must be its product."

The translation of the 'Essence of Christianity' was also published by Mr. Chapman in 1854. It appeared in his 'Quarterly Series,' destined " to consist of works by learned and profound thinkers, embracing the subjects of theology, philosophy, biblical criticism, and the history of opinion." Probably because her former translation had been so eminently successful, Miss Evans received fifty pounds for her present work. But there was no demand for it in England, and Mr. Chapman lost heavily by its publication.

About the same period Miss Evans also translated Spinoza's *De Deo* for the benefit of an inquiring friend. . But her English version of the 'Ethics' was not undertaken till the year 1854, after she had left her home at Foleshill. In applying herself to the severe labour of rendering one philosophical work after another into English, Miss Evans, no doubt, was bent on elucidating for herself some of the most vital problems which engage the mind when once it has shaken itself free from purely traditional beliefs, rather than on securing for herself any pecuniary advantages. But her admirable translations attracted the attention of the like-minded, and she became gradually known to some of the most distinguished men of the time.

Unfortunately her father's health now began to fail, causing her no little pain and anxiety. At some period during his illness she stayed with him in the Isle of Wight, for in a letter to Mrs. Bray, written many years afterwards, she says, "The 'Sir Charles Grandison' you are reading must be the series of little fat volumes you lent me to carry to the Isle of Wight, where I read it at every interval when my father did not want me, and was sorry that the long novel was not longer. It is a solace to hear of any one's reading and enjoying Richardson. We have fallen on an evil generation who would not read 'Clarissa' even in an abridged form. The French have been its most enthusiastic admirers, but I don't know whether their present admiration is more than traditional, like their set phrases about their own classics."

During the last year of her father's life his daughter was also in the habit of reading Scott's novels aloud to him for several hours of each day; she must thus have become deeply versed in his manner of telling the stories in which she continued to delight all her life; and in speaking of the widening of our sympathies which a picture of human life by a great artist is calculated to produce, even in the most trivial and selfish, she gives as an instance Scott's description of Luckie Mucklebackit's cottage, and his story of the 'Two Drovers.'

But a heavy loss now befell Marian Evans in the death of her father, which occurred in 1849. Long afterwards nothing seemed to afford consolation to

E

her grief. For eight years these two had kept house together, and the deepest mutual affection had always subsisted between them. Marian ever treasured her father's memory. As George Eliot she loved to recall in her works everything associated with him in her childhood ; those happy times when, standing between her father's knees, she used to be driven by him to "outlying hamlets, whose groups of inhabitants were as distinctive to my imagination as if they belonged to different regions of the globe." Miss Evans, however, was not suffered to mourn uncomforted. The tender friends who cared for her as a sister, now planned a tour to the Continent in hopes that the change of scene and associations would soften her grief.

So they started on their travels, going to Switzerland and Italy by the approved route, which in those days was not so hackneyed as it now is. To so penetrating an observer as Miss Evans there must have been an infinite interest in this first sight of the Continent. But the journey did not seem to dispel her grief, and she continued in such very low spirits that Mrs. Bray almost regretted having taken her abroad so soon after her bereavement. Her terror, too, at the giddy passes which they had to cross, with precipices yawning on either hand—so that it seemed as if a false step must send them rolling into the abyss—was so overpowering that the sublime spectacle of the snow-clad Alps seemed comparatively to produce but little impression on her. Her moral triumph over this constitutional timidity, when any special occasion arose, was all the more remarkable. One day when crossing the Col de Balme from Martigny to Chamounix, one of the side-saddles was found to be badly fitted, and would keep turning round, to the risk of the rider, if not very careful, slipping off at any moment. Marian, however, insisted on having this defective saddle in spite of the protest of Mrs. Bray, who felt quite guilty whenever they came to any perilous places.

How different is this timidity from George Sand's hardy spirit of enterprise! No one who has read that captivating book, her *Lettres d'un Voyageur*, can forget the great Frenchwoman's description of a Swiss expedition, during which, while encumbered with two young children, she seems to have borne all the perils, fatigues, and privations of a toilsome ascent with the hardihood of a mountaineer. But it should not be forgotten that Miss Marian Evans was just then in a peculiarly nervous, and excitable condition, and her frequent fits of weeping were a source of pain to her anxious fellow-travellers. She had, in fact, been so assiduous in attendance on her sick father, that she was physically broken down for a time. Under these circumstances an immediate return to England seemed unadvisable, and, when her friends started on their homeward journey, it was decided that Marian should remain behind at Geneva.

Here, amid scenes so intimately associated with genius—where the "self-torturing sophist, wild Rousseau," placed the home of his '*Nouvelle Héloïse*,' and the octogenarian Voltaire spent the serene Indian summer of his stirring career; where Gibbon wrote his 'History of the Decline and Fall of the Roman Empire;' where Byron and Shelley sought refuge from the hatred of their countrymen, and which Madame de Staël complainingly exchanged for her beloved Rue du Bac—here the future author of

'Romola' and 'Middlemarch' gradually recovered under the sublime influences of Nature's healing beauties.

For about eight months Miss Evans lived at a boarding-house, "Le Plongeau," near Geneva. But she was glad to find a quieter retreat in the family of an artist, M. d'Albert, becoming much attached to him and his wife. Established in one of the lofty upper stories of this pleasant house, with the blue shimmering waters of the lake glancing far below, and the awful heights of Mont Blanc solemnly dominating the entire landscape, she not only loved to prosecute her studies, but, in isolation from mankind, to plan glorious schemes for their welfare. During this stay she drank deep of Rousseau, whose works, especially *Les Confessions*, made an indelible impression on her. And when inciting a friend to study French, she remarked that it was worth learning that language, if only to read him. At the same period Marian probably became familiarised with the magnificent social utopias of St. Simon, Proudhon, and other French writers. Having undergone a kind of mental revolution herself not so long ago, she must have felt some sympathy with the thrilling hopes of liberty which had agitated the states of Western Europe in 1849. But, as I have already pointed out, her nature had conservative leanings. She believed in progress only as the result of evolution, not revolution. And in one of her most incisive essays, entitled 'The National History of German Life,' she finely points out the "notable failure of revolutionary attempts conducted from the point of view of abstract democratic and socialistic theories." In the same article she draws a striking parallel between the growth of language and that of political institutions, contending that it would be as unsatisfactory to "construct a universal language on a rational basis" —one that had "no uncertainty, no whims of idiom, no cumbrous forms, no fitful shimmer of many-hued significance, no hoary archaisms 'familiar with forgotten years'"—as abruptly to alter forms of government which are nothing, in fact, but the result of historical growth, systematically embodied by society.

Besides the fascinations of study, and the outward glory of nature, the charm of social intercourse was not wanting to this life at Geneva. In M. D'Albert, a very superior man, gentle, refined, and of unusual mental attainments, she found a highly desirable daily companion. He was an artist by profession, and it is whispered that he suggested some of the traits in the character of the delicate-minded Philip Wakem in the 'Mill on the Floss.' The only portrait in oils which exists of George Eliot is one painted by M. D'Albert at this interesting time of her life. She inspired him, like most people who came into personal contact with her, with the utmost admiration and regard, and, wishing to be of some service, he escorted Miss Evans to England on her return thither. Curiously enough, M. D'Albert subsequently translated one of her works, probably 'Adam Bede,' without in the least suspecting who its real author was.

It is always a shock when vital changes have occurred in one's individual lot to return to a well-known place, after an absence of some duration, to find it wearing the same unchangeable aspect. One expects somehow that fields and streets and houses would show some alteration corresponding to that within ourselves. But already from a distance the twin spires of Coventry, familiar as household words to the Warwickshire girl, greeted the eyes of the returning traveller. In spite of all love for her native spot of earth, this was a heavy time to Marian Evans. Her father was dead, the home where she had dwelt as mistress for so many years broken up, the present appearing blank and comfortless, the future uncertain and vaguely terrifying. The question now was where she should live, what she should do, to what purposes turn the genius whose untried and partially unsuspected powers were darkly agitating her whole being.

As has been already said, Marian Evans had a highly complex nature, compounded of many contradictory impulses, which, though gradually brought into harmony as life matured, were always pulling her, in those days, in different directions. Thus, though she possessed strong family affections, she could not help feeling that to go and take up her abode in the house of some relative, where life resolved itself into a monotonous recurrence of petty considerations, something after the Glegg pattern, would be little short of crucifixion to her, and, however deep her attachment for her native soil may have been, she yet sighed passionately to break away from its associations, and to become "a wanderer and a pilgrim on the face of the earth."

For some little time after her return from abroad Marian took up her residence with her brother and his family. But the children who had toddled hand-in-hand in the fields together had now diverged so widely that no memories of a mutual past could bridge over the chasm that divided them. Under these circumstances the family at Rosehill pressed her to make their home permanently hers, and for about a year, from 1850 to 1851, she became the member of a household in fullest sympathy with her. Here Mr. Bray's many-sided mental activity and genial brightness of disposition, and his wife's exquisite goodness of heart, must have helped to soothe and cheer one whose delicately strung nature was just then nearly bending under the excessive strain of thought and feeling she had gone through. One person, indeed, was so struck by the grave sadness generally affecting her, that it seemed to him as if her coming took all the sunshine out of the day. But whether grave or gay, whether meditative or playful, her conversation exercised a spell over all who came within its reach.

In the pleasant house at Rosehill distinguished guests were constantly coming and going, so that there was no lack of the needed intellectual friction supplied by clever and original talk. Here in a pleasant garden, planted with rustling acacia trees, and opening on a wide prospect of richly-wooded, undulating country, with the fitful brightness of English skies overhead, and a smooth-shaven lawn to walk or recline upon, many were the topics discussed by men who had made, or were about to make, their mark. Froude was known there. George Combe discussed with his host the principles of phrenology, at that time claiming "its thousands of disciples." Ralph Waldo Emerson, on a lecturing tour in this country, while on a brief visit, made Marian's acquaintance, and was observed by Mrs. Bray engaged in eager talk with her. Suddenly she

saw him start.   Something said by this quiet, gentle-
mannered girl had evidently given him a shock of
surprise. Afterwards, in conversation with her friends,
he spoke of her "great calm soul."   This is no doubt
an instance of the intense sympathetic adaptiveness
of Miss Evans.   If great, she was not by any means
calm at this period, but inwardly deeply perturbed,
yet her nature, with subtlest response, reflected the
transcendental calm of the philosopher when brought
within his atmosphere.

George Dawson, the popular lecturer, and Mr.
Flower, were more intimately associated with the
Rosehill household.   The latter, then living at Strat-
ford-on-Avon, where he was wont to entertain a vast
number of people, especially Americans, who make
pilgrimages to Shakespeare's birthplace, is known to
the world as the benevolent denouncer of "bits and
bearing-reins."   One day this whole party went to
hear George Dawson, who had made a great sensation at Birmingham, preach one of his thrilling
sermons from the text "And the common people
heard him gladly."   George Eliot, alluding to these
days as late as 1876, says, in a letter to Mrs. Bray:

"George Dawson was strongly associated for me
with Rosehill, not to speak of the General Baptist
Chapel, where we all heard him preach for the first
time (to us). ... I have a vivid recollection of an
evening when Mr. and Mrs. F— dined at your
house with George Dawson, when he was going to
lecture at the Mechanics' Institute, and you felt
compassionately towards him, because you thought
the rather riotous talk was a bad preface to his lecture.
We have a Birmingham friend, whose acquaintance
we made many years ago in Weimar, and from him

I have occasionally had some news of Mr. Dawson.
I feared, what you mention, that his life has been a
little too strenuous in these latter years."

On the evening alluded to in this letter Mr. Dawson
was dining at Mrs. Bray's house before giving his
lecture on ' John Wesley,' at the Mechanics' Institute.
His rich sarcasm and love of fun had exhilarated
the whole company, and not content with merely
"riotous talk," George Dawson and Mr. Flower turned
themselves into lions and wild cats for the amusement
of the children, suddenly pouncing out from under the
table-cloth, with hideous roarings and screechings, till
the hubbub became appalling, joined to the delighted
half-frightened exclamations of the little ones. Mr.
Dawson did the lions, and Mr. Flower, who had made
personal acquaintance with the wild cats in the back-
woods of America, was inimitable in their peculiar
pounce and screech.

Thus amid studies and pleasant friendly intercourse
did the days pass at Roschill. Still Marian Evans
was restless, tormented, frequently in tears, perhaps
unconsciously craving a wider sphere, and more defi-
nitely recognised position. However strenuously she,
at a maturer time of life, inculcated the necessity of
resignation, she had not then learned to resign herself.
And now a change was impending—a change which,
fraught with the most important consequences, was
destined to give a new direction to the current of her
life. Dr. John Chapman invited her to assist him
in the editorship of the *Westminster Review*, which
passed at that time into his hands from John Mill.
They had already met, when Marian was passing
through London on her way to the Continent, on
some matter of business or other connected with

one of her translations. Dr. Chapman's proposition
was accepted ; and although Marian suffered keenly
from the wrench of parting with her friends, the
prompting to work out her powers to the full over-
came the clinging of affection, and in the spring
of 1851 she left Rosehill behind her and came to
London.

CHAPTER V.

THE 'WESTMINSTER REVIEW.'

DR. and Mrs. Chapman were at this time in the habit of· admitting a few select boarders, chiefly engaged in literary pursuits, to their large house in the Strand, and Miss Evans, at their invitation, made her home with them. Thus she found herself at once in the centre of a circle consisting of some of the most advanced thinkers and brilliant *littérateurs* of the day ; a circle which, partly consisting of contributors to the *Westminster Review*, was strongly imbued with scientific tendencies, being particularly partial to the doctrines of Positive Philosophy.

Those were in truth the palmy days of the *Westminster Review*. Herbert Spencer, G. H. Lewes, John Oxenford, James and Harriet Martineau, Charles Bray, George Combe, and Professor Edward Forbes were among the writers that made it the leading expositor of the philosophic and scientific thought of the age. It occupied a position something midway between that of the *Nineteenth Century* and the *Fortnightly*. Scorning, like the latter, to pander to the frivolous tastes of the majority, it appealed to the most thoughtful and enlightened section of the reading public, giving especial prominence to the philosophy of the Comtist School ; and while not so fashionable ·

as the *Nineteenth Century*, it could boast among its
contributors names quite as famous, destined as
they were to become the foremost of their time and
country. With this group of illustrious writers Miss
Evans was now associated, and the articles she contributed from the year 1852 to 1858 are among the
most brilliant examples of periodical literature. The
first notice by her pen is a brief review of Carlyle's
'Life of Sterling' for January 1852, and judging from
internal evidence, as regards style and method of
treatment, the one on Margaret Fuller, in the next
number, must be by the same hand.

To the biographer there is a curious interest in
what she says in her first notice about this kind of
literature, and it would be well for the world if writers
were to lay it more generally to heart. "We have
often wished that genius would incline itself more
frequently to the task of the biographer, that when
some great or good personage dies, instead of the
dreary three- or five-volumed compilations of letter,
and diary, and detail, little to the purpose, which two-
thirds of the public have not the chance, nor the other
third the inclination, to read, we could have a real
"life," setting forth briefly and vividly the man's inward and outward struggles, aims, and achievements,
so as to make clear the meaning which his experience
has for his fellows. A few such lives (chiefly autobiographies) the world possesses, and they have,
perhaps, been more influential on the formation of
character than any other kind of reading." Then
again, speaking of the 'Memoirs of Margaret Fuller,'
she remarks, in reference to the same topic, "The old-
world biographies present their subjects generally as
broken fragments of humanity, noticeable because of

their individual peculiarities, the new-world biographies present their subjects rather as organic portions of society."

George Eliot's estimate of Margaret Fuller (for there can be little doubt that it is hers) possesses too rare an interest for readers not to be given here in her own apposite and pungent words : " We are at a loss whether to regard her as the parent or child of New England Transcendentalism.   Perhaps neither the one nor the other.   It was essentially an intellectual, moral, spiritual regeneration—a renewing of the whole man—a kindling of his aspirations after full development of faculty and perfect symmetry of being.   Of this sect Margaret Fuller was the priestess.   In conversation she was as copious and oracular as Coleridge, brilliant as Sterling, pungent and paradoxical as Carlyle ; gifted with the inspired powers of a Pythoness, she saw into the hearts and over the heads of all who came near her, and, but for a sympathy as boundless as her self-esteem, she would have despised the whole human race!   Her frailty in this respect was no secret either to herself or her friends. . . . . We must say that from the time she became a mother till the final tragedy when she perished with her husband and child within sight of her native shore, she was an altered woman, and evinced a greatness of soul and heroism of character so grand and subduing, that we feel disposed to extend to her whole career the admiration and sympathy inspired by the closing scenes.

" While her reputation was at its height in the literary circles of Boston and New York, she was so self-conscious that her life seemed to be a studied act, rather than a spontaneous growth ; but this was the

mere flutter on the surface; the well was deep, and
the spring genuine; and it is creditable to her friends,
as well as to herself, that such at all times was their
belief."

In this striking summing-up of a character, the
penetrating observer of human nature—taking in at a
glance and depicting by a few masterly touches all
that helps to make up a picture of the real living
being—begins to reveal herself.

These essays in the *Westminster Review* are not
only capital reading in themselves, but are, of course,
doubly attractive to us because they let out opinions,
views, judgments of things and authors, which we
should never otherwise have known. -Marian Evans
had not yet hidden herself behind the mask of George
Eliot, and in many of these wise and witty utterances
of hers we are admitted behind the scenes of her
mind, so to speak, and see her in her own undisguised
person — before she had assumed the *rôle* of the
novelist, showing herself to the world mainly through
her dramatic impersonations.

In these articles, written in the fresh maturity
of her powers, we learn what George Eliot thought
about many subjects; we learn who were her favourite
authors in fiction; what opinions she held on art and
poetry; what was her attitude towards the political and
social questions of the day; what was her conception
of human life in general. There is much here, no
doubt, that one might have been prepared to find,
but a good deal, too, that comes upon one with the
freshness of surprise.

A special interest attaches naturally to what she
has to say about her own branch of art—the novel.
Though she had probably no idea that she was herself

destined to become one of the great masters of fiction,
she had evidently a special predilection for works of
that kind, noticeable because hitherto her bent might
have appeared almost exclusively towards philosophy.
To the three-volume circulating-library novel of the
ordinary stamp she is merciless in her sarcasm. One
of her most pithy articles of this time, or rather later,
its date being 1856, is directed against " Silly Novels
by Lady Novelists." "These," she says, "consist of the
frothy, the prosy, the pious, or the pedantic. But it is
a mixture of all these—a composite order of feminine
fatuity, that produces the largest class of such novels,
which we shall distinguish as the *mind and millinery*
species. We had imagined that destitute women
turned novelists, as they turned governesses, because
they had no other 'ladylike' means of getting their
bread. Empty writing was excused by an empty
stomach, and twaddle was consecrated by tears. . . .
It is clear that they write in elegant boudoirs, with
violet-coloured ink and a ruby pen, that they must
be entirely indifferent to publishers' accounts, and in-
experienced in every form of poverty except poverty
of brains."

After finding fault with what she sarcastically calls
the *white neck-cloth* species of novel, "a sort of medical
sweetmeat for Low Church young ladies," she adds,
"The real drama of Evangelicalism, and it has abun-
dance of fine drama for any one who has genius
enough to discern and reproduce it, lies among the
middle and lower classes. Why can we not have
pictures of religious life among the industrial classes
in England, as interesting as Mrs. Stowe's pictures of
religious life among the negroes?"

She who asked that question was herself destined,

a few years later, to answer her own demand in most triumphant fashion. Already here and there we find hints and suggestions of the vein that was to be so fully worked out in 'Scenes of Clerical Life' and 'Adam Bede.' Her intimate knowledge of English country life, and the hold it had on her imagination, every now and then eats its way to the surface of her writings, and stands out amongst its surrounding matter with a certain unmistakable native force. After censuring the lack of reality with which peasant life is commonly treated in art, she makes the following apposite remarks, suggested by her own experience: "The notion that peasants are joyous, that the typical moment to represent a man in a smock-frock is when he is cracking a joke and showing a row of sound teeth, that cottage matrons are usually buxom, and village children necessarily rosy and merry, are prejudices difficult to dislodge from the artistic mind which looks for its subjects into literature instead of life. The painter is still under the influence of idyllic literature, which has always expressed the imagination of the town-bred rather than the truth of rustic life. Idyllic ploughmen are jocund when they drive their team afield ; idyllic shepherds make bashful love under hawthorn bushes ; idyllic villagers dance in the chequered shade and refresh themselves not immoderately with spicy nut-brown ale. But no one who has seen much of actual ploughmen thinks them jocund, no one who is well acquainted with the English peasantry can pronounce them merry. The slow gaze, in which no sense of beauty beams, no humour twinkles ; the slow utterance, and the heavy slouching walk, remind one rather of that melancholy animal the camel, than of the sturdy countryman, with striped stockings, red waistcoat, and hat aside, who represents the traditional English peasant. Observe a company of haymakers. When you see them at a distance tossing up the forkfuls of hay in the golden light, while the wagon creeps slowly with its increasing burden over the meadow, and the bright green space which tells of work done gets larger and larger, you pronounce the scene 'smiling,' and you think these companions in labour must be as bright and cheerful as the picture to which they give animation. Approach nearer and you will find haymaking time is a time for joking, especially if there are women among the labourers; but the coarse laugh that bursts out every now and then, and expresses the triumphant taunt, is as far as possible from your conception of idyllic merriment. That delicious effervescence of the mind which we call fun has no equivalent for the northern peasant, except tipsy revelry; the only realm of fancy and imagination for the English clown exists at the bottom of the third quart pot.

"The conventional countryman of the stage, who picks up pocket-books and never looks into them, and who is too simple even to know that honesty has its opposite, represents the still lingering mistake, that an unintelligible dialect is a guarantee for ingenuousness, and that slouching shoulders indicate an upright disposition. It is quite sure that a thresher is likely to be innocent of any adroit arithmetical cheating, but he is not the less likely to carry home his master's corn in his shoes and pocket; a reaper is not given to writing begging-letters, but he is quite capable of cajoling the dairy-maid into filling his small-beer bottle with ale. The selfish instincts are not subdued by the sight of buttercups, nor is integrity in the least established by that classic rural occupation, sheep-washing. To make men moral something more is requisite than to turn them out to grass."

Every one must see that this is the essay writing of a novelist rather than of a moral philosopher. The touches are put on with the vigour of a Velasquez. Balzac, or Flaubert, or that most terrible writer of the modern French school of fiction, the author of 'Le Sabot Rouge,' never described peasant life with more downright veracity. In the eyes of Miss Evans this quality of veracity is the most needful of all for the artist. Because "a picture of human life, such as a great artist can give, surprises even the trivial and the selfish into that attention to what is apart from themselves, which may be called the raw material of sentiment." For "art is the nearest thing to life; it is a mode of amplifying experience and extending our contact with our fellow-men beyond the bounds of our personal lot. All the more sacred is the task of the artist when he undertakes to paint the life of the People. Falsification here is far more pernicious than in the more artificial aspects of life. It is not so very serious that we should have false ideas about evanescent fashions—about the manners and conversation of beaux and duchesses; but it *is* serious that our sympathy with the perennial joys and struggles, the toil, the tragedy, and the humour in the life of our more heavily laden fellow-men should be perverted, and turned towards a false object instead of a true one."

George Eliot afterwards faithfully adhered to the canons fixed by the critic. Whether this consciousness of a moral purpose was altogether a gain to her art may be more fitly discussed in connection with the analysis of her works of fiction. It is only needful to point out here how close and binding she wished to make the union between ethics and æsthetics.

Almost identical views concerning fundamental laws of Art are discussed in an equally terse, vigorous, and pictorial manner in an article called 'Realism in Art : Recent German Fiction.' This article, however, is not by George Eliot, but by George Henry Lewes. It was published in October 1858, and appeared after their joint sojourn in Germany during the spring and summer of that year. I think that if one carefully compares ' Realism in Art' with George Eliot's other articles, there appears something like a marriage of their respective styles in this paper. It seems probable that Lewis, with his flexible adaptiveness, had come under the influence of George Eliot's powerful intellect, and that many of the views he expresses here at the same time render George Eliot's, as they frequently appear, identical with hers. In the article in question the manner as well as the matter has a certain suggestion of the novelist's style. For example she frequently indicates the quality of human speech by its resemblance to musical sounds. She is fond of speaking of "the *staccato* tones of a voice," " an *adagio* of utter indifference," and in the above-mentioned essay there are such expressions as the "stately *largo*" of good German prose. Again, in the article in question, we find the following satirical remarks about the slovenly prose of the generality of German writers: "To be gentlemen of somewhat slow, sluggish minds is perhaps their misfortune ; but to be writers deplorably deficient in the first principles of composition is assuredly their fault. Some men pasture on platitudes, as oxen upon meadow-grass ; they are at home on a dead-level of common-place, and do not desire to be irradiated by a felicity of expression." And in another passage to the same effect the author says sarcastically, " Graces are gifts : it can no more be required of a professor that he should write with felicity than that he should charm all beholders with his personal appearance ; but litera-ture requires that he should write intelligibly and carefully, as society requires that he should wash his face and button his waistcoat." Some of these stric-tures are very similar in spirit to what George Eliot had said in her review of Heinrich Heine, published in 1856, where complaining of the general cumbrous-ness of German writers, she makes the following cutting remark : " A German comedy is like a German sentence : you see. no reason in its structure why it should ever come to an end, and you accept the conclusion as an arrangement of Providence rather than of the author."

A passage in this article, which exactly tallies with George Eliot's general remarks on Art, must not be omitted here. "Art is a representation of Reality—a Representation inasmuch as it is not the thing itself, but only represents it, must necessarily be limited by the nature of its medium. . . . Realism is thus the basis of all Art, and its antithesis is not Idealism but Falsism. . . . To misrepresent the forms of ordinary life is no less an offence than to misrepre-sent the forms of ideal life : a pug-nosed Apollo, or Jupiter in a great-coat, would not be more truly shocking to an artistic mind than are those senseless falsifications of Nature into which incompetence is

led under the pretence of 'beautifying' Nature.
Either give us true peasants or leave them un-
touched; either paint no drapery at all, or paint it
with the utmost fidelity; either keep your people
silent, or make them speak the idiom of their
class."

Among German novelists (or rather writers of short
stories), Paul Heyse is one of the few who is singled
out for special praise in this review. And it is curious
that there should be a tale by this eminent author
called 'The Lonely Ones' (which also appeared in
1858), in which an incident occurs forcibly recalling
the catastrophe of Grandcourt's death in 'Daniel Deronda': the incident—although unskilfully introduced
—of a Neapolitan fisherman whose momentary murderous hesitation to rescue his drowning friend ends
in lifelong remorse for his death.

What makes the article in question particularly
interesting are the allusions to the German tour, which
give it an almost biographical interest. As has been
mentioned already, Mr. Lewes and George Eliot were
travelling in Germany in the spring of 1858, and in
a letter to a friend she writes: "Then we had a
delicious journey to Salzburg, and from thence
through the Salz-Kammergut to Vienna, from Vienna
to Prague, and from Prague to Dresden, where we
spent our last six weeks in quiet work and quiet
worship of the Madonna." And in his essay on Art
Mr. G. H. Lewes alludes to the most priceless art-
treasure Dresden contains, "Raphael's marvellous
picture, the Madonna di San Sisto," as furnishing the
most perfect illustration of what he means by Realism
and Idealism. Speaking of the child Jesus he says:
"In the never-to-be-forgotten divine babe, we have

at once the intensest realism of presentation with the highest idealism of conception : the attitude is at once grand, easy and natural ; the face is that of a child, but the child is divine : in those eyes and in that brow there is an indefinable something which, greater than the expression of the angels, grander than that of pope or saint, is to all who see it a perfect *truth ;* we feel that humanity in its highest conceivable form is before us, and that to transcend such a form would be to lose sight of the *human* nature there represented." A similar passage occurs in 'The Mill on the Floss,' where Philip Wakem says: "The greatest of painters only once painted a mysteriously divine child ; he couldn't have told how he did it, and we can't tell why we feel it to be divine."

Enough has probably been quoted from George Eliot's articles to give the reader some idea of her views on art. But they are so rich in happy aphorisms, originality of illustration, and raciness of epithet that they not only deserve attentive study because they were the first fruits of the mind that afterwards gave to the world such noble and perfect works as 'The Mill on the Floss' and 'Silas Marner,' but are well worth attention for their own sake. Indeed nothing in George Eliot's fictions excels the style of these papers. And what a clear, incisive, masterly style it was ! Her prose in those days had a swiftness of movement, an epigrammatic felicity, and a brilliancy of antithesis which we look for in vain in the over-elaborate sentences and somewhat ponderous wit of 'Theophrastus Such.'

A very vapid paper on 'Weimar and its Celebrities,' April 1859, which a writer in the *Academy* attributes to the same hand, I know not on what

authority, does not possess a single attribute that
we are in the habit of associating with the writings
of George Eliot. That an author who, by that
time, had already produced some of her very finest
work, namely, the 'Scenes of Clerical Life,' and
'Adam Bede,' should have been responsible simulta-
neously for the trite commonplaces ventilated in this
article is simply incredible. It is true that Homer is
sometimes found nodding, and the right-hand of the
greatest master may forget its cunning, but would
George Eliot in her most abject moments have been
capable of penning such a sentence as this in connection with Goethe? "Would not Fredricka or Lili
have been a more genial companion than Christina
Vulpius for that great poet of whom his native land
is so justly proud?" It is not worth while to point
out other platitudes such as flow spontaneously from
the facile pen of a penny-a-liner; but the consistent
misspelling of every name may be alluded to in
passing. Thus we read "Lily" for "Lely," "Zetter"
for "Zelter," "Quintus Filein" for "Fixlein," "Ein-
sédel" for "Einsiedel," etc. etc. This, in itself, would
furnish no conclusive argument, supposing George
Eliot to have been on the Continent and out of the
way of correcting proofs. But as it happened she
was in England in April 1859, and it is, therefore,
on all grounds impossible that this worthless production should be hers.

Perhaps her two most noteworthy articles are the
one called 'Evangelical Teaching,' published in 1855,
and the other on 'Worldliness and other Worldliness,'
which appeared in 1857. This happy phrase, by the
way, was first used by Coleridge, who says, "As there
is a worldliness or the too much of this life, so there

is another *worldliness* or rather *other worldliness* equally hateful and selfish with *this worldliness.*" These articles are curious because they seem to occupy a midway position between George Eliot's earliest and latest phase of religious belief. But at this period she still felt the recoil from the pressure of a narrowing dogmatism too freshly not to launch back at it some of the most stinging shafts from the armoury of her satire. Not Heine himself, in his trenchant sallies, surpasses the irony with which some of her pages are bristling. To ignore this stage in George Eliot's mental development would be to lose one of the connecting links in her history : a history by no means smooth and uneventful, as some times superficially represented, but full of strong con-trasts, abrupt transitions, outward and inward changes sympathetically charged with all the meaning of this transitional time. Two extracts from the above-mentioned articles will amply testify to what has just been said.

"Given a man with a moderate intellect, a moral standard not higher than the average, some rhetorical affluence and great glibness of speech, what is the career in which, without the aid of birth or money, he may most easily attain power and reputation in English society ? Where is that Goshen of intel-lectual mediocrity in which a smattering of science and learning will pass for profound instruction, where platitudes will be accepted as wisdom, bigoted nar-rowness as holy zeal, unctuous egoism as God-given piety ? Let such a man become an evangelical preacher ; he will then find it possible to reconcile small ability with great ambition, superficial know-ledge with the prestige of erudition, a middling

morale with a high reputation for sanctity. Let him
shun practical extremes, and be ultra only in what is
purely theoretic. Let him be stringent on predestination, but latitudinarian on fasting; unflinching in
insisting on the eternity of punishment, but diffident
of curtailing the substantial comforts of time; ardent
and imaginative on the pre-millenial advent of Christ,
but cold and cautious towards every other infringe-
ment of the *status quo*. Let him fish for souls, not
with the bait of inconvenient singularity, but with the
drag-net of comfortable conformity. Let him be hard
and literal in his interpretation only when he wants
to hurl texts at the heads of unbelievers and adver-
saries, but when the letter of the Scriptures presses
too closely on the genteel Christianity of the nineteenth century, let him use his spiritualising alembic
and disperse it into impalpable ether. Let him preach
less of Christ than of Antichrist; let him be less
definite in showing what sin is than in showing who
is the Man of Sin; less expansive on the blessedness
of faith than on the accursedness of infidelity. Above
all, let him set up as an interpreter of prophecy, rival
'Moore's Almanack' in the prediction of political
events, tickling the interest of hearers who are but
moderately spiritual by showing how the Holy Spirit
has dictated problems and charades for their benefit;
and how, if they are ingenious enough to solve these,
they may have their Christian graces nourished by
learning precisely to whom they may point as 'the
horn that had eyes,' 'the lying prophet,' and the
'unclean spirits.' In this way he will draw men to
him by the strong cords of their passions, made
reason-proof by being baptized with the name of
piety. In this way he may gain a metropolitan pulpit;

the avenues to his church will be as crowded as the
passages to the opera ; he has but to print his pro-
phetic sermons, and bind them in lilac and gold, and
they will adorn the drawing-room table of all evangelical ladies, who will regard as a sort of pious 'light
reading' the demonstration that the prophecy of the
locusts, whose sting is in their tail, is fulfilled in the
fact of the Turkish commander having taken a
horse's tail for his standard, and that the French are
the very frogs predicted in the Revelations."

Even more scathing than this onslaught on a certain type of the popular evangelical preacher, is the
paper on the poet Young, one of the wittiest things
from George Eliot's pen, wherein she castigates with
all her powers of sarcasm and ridicule that class of
believers who cannot vilify this life sufficiently in
order to make sure of the next, and who, in the care
of their own souls, are careless of the world's need.
Her analysis of the 'Night Thoughts' remains one
of the most brilliant criticisms of its kind.   Young's
contempt for this earth, of all of us, and his exaltation of the starry worlds above, especially provoke
his reviewer's wrath.   This frame of mind was
always repulsive to George Eliot, who could never
sufficiently insist on the need of man's concentrating
his love and energy on the life around him.   She
never felt much toleration for that form of aspiration
that would soar to some shadowy infinite beyond the
circle of human fellowship.   One of the most epigrammatic passages in this article is where she says of
Young, " No man can be better fitted for an Established Church.   He personifies completely her nice
balance of temporalities and spiritualities.   He is
equally impressed with the momentousness of death

and of burial fees; he languishes at once for immortal
life and for 'livings;' he has a fervid attachment to
patrons in general, but on the whole prefers the
Almighty. He will teach, with something more than
official conviction, the nothingness of earthly things;
and he will feel something more than private disgust,
if his meritorious efforts in directing men's attention
to another world are not rewarded by substantial
preferment in this. His secular man believes in
cambric bands and silk stockings as characteristic
attire for 'an ornament of religion and virtue;' he
hopes courtiers will never forget to copy Sir Robert
Walpole; and writes begging letters to the king's
mistress. His spiritual man recognizes no motives
more familiar than Golgotha and 'the skies;' it
walks in graveyards, or soars among the stars. . . .
If it were not for the prospect of immortality, he considers it would be wise and agreeable to be indecent,
or to murder one's father; and, heaven apart, it would
be extremely irrational in any man not to be a knave.
Man, he thinks, is a compound of the angel and the
brute; the brute is to be humbled by being reminded
of its 'relation to the stars,' and frightened into mode-
ration by the contemplation of deathbeds and skulls;
the angel is to be developed by vituperating this
world and exalting the next, and by this double
process you get the Christian—'the highest style of
man.' With all this our new-made divine is an unmistakable poet. To a clay compounded chiefly of
the worldling and the rhetorician there is added a
real spark of Promethean fire. He will one day
clothe his apostrophes and objurgations, his astro-
nomical religion and his charnel house morality, in
lasting verse, which will stand, like a Juggernaut

made of gold and jewels, at once magnificent and . repulsive : for this divine is Edward Young, the future author of the ' Night Thoughts.' "

It has seemed appropriate to quote thus largely from these essays, because, never having been re-printed, they are to' all intents and purposes inaccessible to the general reader. Yet they contain much that should not willingly be consigned to the dust and cobwebs, among which obsolete magazines usually sink into oblivion. They may as well be specified here according to their dates. 'Carlyle's Life of Sterling,' January 1852 ; 'Woman in France : Madame de Sablé,' October 1854; 'Evangelical Teaching : Dr. Cumming,' October 1855 ; 'German Wit : Heinrich Heine,' January 1856 ; ' Silly Novels by Lady Novelists,' October 1856; 'The Natural History of German Life,' July 1856 ; and ' Worldli-ness and other Worldliness : the Poet Young,' January 1857.

Miss Evans's main employment on the *West-minster Review* was, however, editorial. She used to write a considerable portion of the summary of contemporary literature at the end of each number. But her co-operation as sub-editor ceased about the close of 1853, when she left Dr. Chapman's house, and went to live in apartments in a small house in Cambridge Terrace, Hyde Park. Marian Evans was not entirely dependent at this time on the proceeds of her literary work, her father having settled the sum of 80*l.* to 100*l.* a year on her for life, the capital of which, however, did not belong to her. She was very generous with her money ; and although her earnings at this time were not considerable, they were partly spent on her poor relations.

CHAPTER VI.

GEORGE HENRY LEWES.

MEANWHILE, these literary labours were pleasantly diversified by frequent visits to her friends at Rosehill and elsewhere. In October 1852, she stayed with Mr. and Mrs. George Combe at Edinburgh, and on her way back was the guest of Harriet Martineau, at her delightfully situated house in Ambleside. Her acquaintance with Mr. Herbert Spencer had ripened into a cordial friendship. They met constantly both in London and in the country, and their intercourse was a source of mutual intellectual enjoyment and profit. As must already have become evident, it is erroneous to suppose that he had any share in the formation of her mind : for as Mr. Herbert Spencer said, in a letter to the *Daily News*, "Our friendship did not commence until 1851 . . . when she was already distinguished by that breadth of culture, and universality of power, which have since made her known to all the world."

In a letter to Miss Phelps, George Eliot touches on this rumour, after alluding in an unmistakable manner to another great contemporary : " I never—to answer one of your questions quite directly—I never had any personal acquaintance with " (naming a prominent Positivist) ; "never saw him to my knowledge, except in the House of Commons; and though I have studied his books, especially his 'Logic' and 'Political Economy,' with much benefit, I have no consciousness of their having made any marked epoch in my life.

"Of Mr. ——'s friendship I have had the honour and advantage for twenty years, but I believe that every main bias of my mind had been taken before I knew him. Like the rest of his readers, I am, of course, indebted to him for much enlargement and clarifying of thought."

But there was another acquaintance which Miss Evans made during the first year of her residence in the Strand, destined to affect the whole future tenor of her life—the acquaintance of Mr. George Henry Lewes, then, like her, a contributor to the *Westminster Review.*

George Henry Lewes was Marian's senior by two years, having been born in London on the 18th of April, 1817. He was educated at Greenwich in a school once possessing a high reputation for thoroughly "grounding" its pupils in a knowledge of the classics. When his education was so far finished, he was placed as clerk in a merchant's office. This kind of occupation proving very distasteful, he turned medical student for a time. Very early in life he was attracted towards philosophy, for at the age of nineteen we find him attending the weekly meetings of a small club, in the habit of discussing metaphysical problems in the parlour of a tavern in Red Lion Square, Holborn. This club, from which the one in 'Daniel Deronda' is supposed to have borrowed many of its features, was the point of junction for a most heterogeneous company. Here, amicably seated round the fire, a speculative tailor would hob and nob with some medical student deep in anatomy ; a second-hand bookseller having devoured the literature on his shelves, ventilated their contents for the general benefit ; and a discursive American mystic was listened to in turn with a Jewish journeyman watchmaker deeply imbued with Spinozism. It is impossible not to connect this Jew, named Cohen, and described as "a man of astonishing subtilty and logical force, no less than of sweet personal worth," with the Mordecai of the novel just mentioned. However wide the after divergencies, here evidently lies the germ. The weak eyes and chest, the grave and gentle demeanour, the whole ideality of character correspond. In some respects G. H. Lewes was the "Daniel Deronda" to this "Mordecai." For he not only loved but venerated his "great calm intellect." "An immense pity," says Mr. Lewes, "a fervid indignation filled me as I came away from his attics in one of the Holborn courts, where I had seen him in the pinching poverty of his home, with his German wife and two little black-eyed children."

To this pure-spirited suffering watchmaker, Lewes owed his first acquaintance with Spinoza. A certain passage, casually cited by Cohen, awakened an eager thirst for more in the youth. The desire to possess himself of Spinoza's works, still in the odour of pestilential heresy, haunted him like a passion. For he himself, then "suffering the social persecution which embitters any departure from accepted creeds," felt in defiant sympathy with all outcasts. On a dreary November evening, the coveted volumes were at length discovered on the dingy shelves of a second-hand bookseller. By the flaring gaslight, young Lewes, with a beating heart, read on the back of a small brown quarto those thrilling words, 'Spinoza: Opera Posthuma!' He was poor in those days, and the price of the volume was twenty shillings, but he would gladly have sacrificed his last sixpence to secure it. Having paid his money with feverish delight, he hurried home in triumph, and immediately set to work on a translation of the 'Ethics,' which, however, he was too impatient to finish.

This little incident is well worth dwelling upon not only as being the first introduction of a notable thinker to philosophy, but as showing the eager impulsive nature of the man. The study of Spinoza led to his publishing an article on his life and works in the *Westminster Review* of 1843, almost the first account of the great Hebrew philosopher which appeared in this country. This article, afterwards incorporated in the 'Biographical History of Philosophy,' formed the nucleus, I believe, of that "admirable piece of synthetic criticism and exposition," as Mr. Frederic Harrison calls it; a work which, according to him, has influenced the thought of the present generation almost more than any single book except Mr. Mill's 'Logic.'

Before the appearance of either article or 'History of Philosophy,' Mr. Lewes went to Germany, and devoted himself to the study of its language and literature, just brought into fashion by Carlyle. Returning to England in 1839, he became one of the most prolific journalists of the day. Witty, brilliant, and many-sided, he seemed pre-eminently fitted by nature for a press writer and *littérateur*. His versatility was so amazing, that a clever talker once said of him: "Lewes can do everything in the world but paint : and he could do that, too, after a week's study."

At this time, besides assisting in the editorship of the *Classical Museum*, he wrote for the *Morning Chronicle*, the *Athenæum*, the *Edinburgh*, *Foreign Quarterly*, *British Quarterly*, *Blackwood*, *Fraser*, and the *Westminster Review*. After publishing 'A Biographical History of Philosophy,' through Mr. Knight's 'Weekly Volumes' in 1846, he wrote two novels, 'Ranthorpe,' and 'Rose, Blanche, and Violet,' which successively appeared in 1847 and 1848. But fiction was not his *forte*, these two productions being singularly crude and immature as compared with his excellent philosophical work. Some jokes in the papers about "rant," killed what little life there was in "Ranthorpe." Nevertheless, Charlotte Brontë, who had some correspondence with Mr. Lewes about 1847, actually wrote about it as follows: "In reading 'Ranthorpe,' I have read a new book, not a reprint, not a reflection of any other book, but a *new book*." Another great writer, Edgar Poe, admired it no less, for he says of the work : " I have lately read it with deep interest, and derived great *consolation* from it also. It relates to the career of a literary man, and gives a just view of the true aims and the true dignity of the literary character."

'The Spanish Drama;' 'The Life of Maximilian Robespierre, with extracts from his unpublished correspondence;' 'The Noble Heart: a Tragedy;' all followed in close succession from the same inexhaustible pen. The last, it was said, proved also a tragedy to the publishers. But not content with writing dramas, Mr. Lewes was also ambitious of the fame of an actor, the theatre having always possessed a strong fascination for him. Already as

G

a child he had haunted the theatres, and now, while
delivering a lecture at the Philosophical Institution in Edinburgh, he shocked its staid *habitués*
not a little by immediately afterwards appearing on
the stage in the character of Shylock : so many, and
seemingly incompatible, were Lewes's pursuits. But
this extreme mobility of mind, this intellectual trip-
ping from subject to subject, retarded the growth of
his popularity. The present mechanical subdivision
of labour has most unfortunately also affected the
judgment passed on literary and artistic products.
Let a man once have written a novel typical of the
manners and ways of a certain class of English society,
or painted a picture with certain peculiar effects of
sea or landscape, or composed a poem affecting the
very trick and language of some bygone mediæval
singer, he will be doomed, to the end of his days, to
do the same thing over and over again, *ad nauseam.*
Nothing can well be more deadening to any vigorous
mental life, and Mr. Lewes set a fine example of
intellectual disinterestedness in sacrificing immediate
success to the free play of a most variously endowed
nature.

The public too was a gainer by this. For the life
of Goethe could not have been made the rich, com-
prehensive, many-sided biography it is, had Mr. Lewes
himself not tried his hand at such a variety of subjects.
This life, begun in 1845, the result partly of his
sojourn in Germany, did not appear in print until
1855. Ultimately destined to a great and lasting
success, the MS. of the 'Life of Goethe' was igno-
miniously sent from one publisher to another, until
at last Mr. David Nutt, of the Strand, showed his
acumen by giving it to the reading world.

Some years before the publication of this biography Mr. Lewes had also been one of the founders of that able, but unsuccessful weekly, the *Leader*, of which he was the literary editor from 1849 to 1854. Many of his articles on Auguste Comte were originally written for this paper, and afterwards collected into a volume for Bohn's series. Indeed, after Mr. John Stuart Mill, he is to be regarded as the earliest exponent of Positivism in England. He not only considered the '*Cours de Philosophie Positive*' the greatest work of this century, but believed it would "form one of the mighty landmarks in the history of opinion. No one before M. Comte," he says, "ever dreamed of treating social problems otherwise than upon theological or metaphysical methods. He first showed how possible, nay, how imperative, it was that social questions should be treated on the same footing with all other scientific questions. This being his object, he was forced to detect the law of mental evolution before he could advance. This law is the law of historical progression." But while Mr. Lewes, with his talent for succinct exposition, helped more than any other Englishman to disseminate the principles of Comte's philosophy in this country, he was at the same time violently opposed to his '*Politique Positive*,' with its schemes of social reorganisation

Even so slight a survey as this must show the astonishing discursiveness of Mr. Lewes's intellect. By the time he was thirty he had already tried his hand at criticism, fiction, biography, the drama, and philosophy. He had enlarged his experience of human nature by foreign travel; he had addressed audiences from the lecturer's platform; he had en-

joyed the perilous sweets of editing a newspaper; he
had even, it is said, played the harlequin in a company
of strolling actors. Indeed, Mr. Thackeray was once
heard to say that it would not surprise him to meet
Lewes in Piccadilly, riding on a white elephant; whilst
another wit likened him to the Wandering Jew, as
you could never tell where he was going to turn up,
or what he was going to do next.

In this discursiveness of intellect he more nearly
resembled the Encyclopedists of the 18th century
than the men of his own time. Indeed his personal appearance, temperament, manners, general
tone of thought, seemed rather to be those of a
highly-accomplished foreigner than of an Englishman.
He was a lightly-built, fragile man, with bushy curly
hair, and a general shagginess of beard and eyebrow
not unsuggestive of a Skye terrier. For the rest, he
had a prominent mouth and grey, deeply-set eyes
under an ample, finely-proportioned forehead. Vola-
tile by nature, somewhat wild and lawless in his talk,
he in turn delighted and shocked his friends by the
gaiety, recklessness, and genial *abandon* of his manners
and conversation. His companionship was singularly
stimulating, for the commonest topic served him as a
starting-point for the lucid development of some pet
philosophical theory. In this gift of making abstruse
problems intelligible, and difficult things easy, he
had some resemblance to the late W. K. Clifford,
with his magical faculty of illuminating the most
abstruse subjects by his vivid directness of exposition.

As Lewes's life was so soon to be closely united
to that of Marian Evans, this cursory sketch of

his career will not seem inappropriate. At the time they met at Dr. Chapman's house, Mr. Lewes, who had married early in life, found his conjugal relations irretrievably spoiled. How far the blame of this might attach to one side or to the other does not concern us here. Enough that in the intercourse with a woman of such astonishing intellect, varied acquirements, and rare sympathy, Mr. Lewes discovered a community of ideas and a moral support that had been sadly lacking to his existence hitherto.

In many ways these two natures, so opposite in character, disposition, and tone of mind, who, from such different starting-points, had reached the same standpoint, seemed to need each other for the final fruition and utmost development of what was best in each. A crisis was now impending in Marian's life. She was called upon to make her private judgment a law unto herself, and to shape her actions, not according to the recognised moral standard of her country, but in harmony with her own convictions of right and wrong. From a girl, it appears, she had held independent views about marriage, strongly advocating the German divorce laws. On the appearance of ' Jane Eyre,' when every one was talking of this book and praising the exemplary conduct of Jane in her famous interview with Rochester, Marian Evans, then only four-and-twenty, remarked to a friend that in his position she considered him justified in contracting a fresh marriage. And in an article on Madame de Sablé, written as early as 1854, there is this significant passage in reference to the "laxity of opinion and practice with regard to the marriage-tie in France." " Heaven

forbid," she writes, "that we should enter on a defence
of French morals, most of all in relation to marriage!
But it is undeniable that unions formed in the maturity
of thought and feeling, and grounded only on inherent
fitness and mutual attraction, tended to bring women
into more intelligent sympathy with man, and to
heighten and complicate their share in the political
drama.   The quiescence and security of the conjugal
relation are, doubtless, favourable to the manifestation
of the highest qualities by persons who have already
attained a high standard of culture, but rarely foster
a passion sufficient to rouse all the faculties to aid in
winning or retaining its beloved object—to convert
indolence into activity, indifference into ardent parti-
sanship, dulness into perspicuity."

Such a union, formed in the full maturity of thought
and feeling, was now contracted by Marian Evans
and George Henry Lewes.   Legal union, however,
there could be none, for though virtually separated
from his wife, Mr. Lewes could not get a divorce.   Too
little has as yet transpired concerning this important
step to indicate more than the bare outline of
events.   Enough that Mr. Lewes appears to have
written a letter in which, after a full explanation
of his circumstances, he used all his powers of
persuasion to win Miss Evans for his life-long companion ; that she consented, after having satisfied
her conscience that in reality she was not injuring
the claims of others ; and that henceforth she bore
Mr. Lewes's name, and became his wife in every
sense but the legal one.

This proceeding caused the utmost consternation
amongst her acquaintances, especially amongst her

friends at Roschill. The former intimate and affectionate intercourse with Mrs. Bray and her sister was only gradually restored, and only after they had come to realise how perfectly her own conscience had been consulted and satisfied in the matter. Miss Hennell, who had already entered on the scheme of religious doctrine which ever since she has been setting forth in her printed works, "swerved nothing from her own principles that the maintenance of a conventional form of marriage (remoulded to the demands of the present age) is essentially attached to all religion, and pre-eminently so to the religion of the future."

In thus defying public opinion, and forming a connection in opposition to the laws of society, George Eliot must have undergone some trials and sufferings peculiarly painful to one so shrinkingly sensitive as herself. Conscious of no wrong-doing, enjoying the rare happiness of completest intellectual fellowship in the man she loved, the step she had taken made a gap between her kindred and herself which could not but gall her clinging, womanly nature. To some of her early companions, indeed, who had always felt a certain awe at the imposing gravity of her manners, this dereliction from what appeared to them the path of duty was almost as startling and unexpected as if they had seen the heavens falling down.

How far the individual can ever be justified in following the dictates of his private judgment, in opposition to the laws and prevalent opinions of his time and country, must remain a question no less difficult than delicate of decision. It is precisely the point where the highest natures and the lowest sometimes apparently meet; since to act in opposition to custom may be due to the loftiest motives—may be the spiritual exaltation of the reformer, braving social ostracism for the sake of an idea, or may spring, on the other hand, from purely rebellious promptings of an anti-social egoism, which recognises no law higher than that of personal gratification. At the same time, it seems, that no progress could well be made in the evolution of society without these departures on the part of individuals from the well-beaten tracks, for even the failures help eventually towards a fuller recognition of what is beneficial and possible of attainment. Mary Wollstonecraft Shelley, George Sand, the New England Transcendentalists, with their communistic experiment at Brooke Farm, all more or less strove to be path-finders to a better and happier state of society. George Eliot, however, hardly belonged to this order of mind. Circumstances prompted her to disregard one of the most binding laws of society, yet, while she considered herself justified in doing so, her sympathies were, on the whole, more enlisted in the state of things as they are than as they might be. It is certainly curious that the woman, who in her own life had followed such an independent course, severing herself in many ways from her past with all its traditional sanctities, should yet so often inculcate the very opposite teaching in her works—should inculcate an almost slavish adherence to whatever surroundings, beliefs, and family ties a human being may be born to.

I need only add here that Mr. Lewes and Marian

went to Germany soon after forming this union, which, only ending by death, gave to each what had hitherto been lacking in their lives. Many marriages solemnised in a church, and ushered in with all the ostentation of *trousseau*, bridesmaids, and wedding break- fast, are indeed less essentially such in all the deeper human aspects which this relation implies, than the one contracted in this informal manner. Indeed, to those who saw them together, it seemed as if they could never be apart. Yet, while so entirely at one, each respected the other's in- dividuality, his own, at the same time, gaining in strength by the contact. Mr. Lewes's mer- curial disposition now assumed a stability greatly enhancing his brilliant talents, and for the first time facilitating that concentration of intellect so necessary for the production of really lasting philosophic work. On the other hand, George Eliot's still dormant faculties were roused and stimulated to the utmost by the man to whom this union with her formed the most memorable year of his life. By his enthusiastic belief in her he gave her the only thing she wanted— a thorough belief in herself. Indeed, he was more than a husband : he was, as an intimate friend once pithily remarked, a very mother to her. Tenderly watching over her delicate health, cheering the grave tenor of her thoughts by his inexhaustible buoy- ancy, jealously shielding her from every adverse breath of criticism, Mr. Lewes in a manner created the spiritual atmosphere in which George Eliot could best put forth all the flowers and fruits of her genius.

In joining her life with that of Mr. Lewes, the care

of his three children devolved upon George Eliot, who henceforth showed them the undeviating love and tenderness of a mother. One of the sons had gone out to Natal as a young man, and contracted a fatal disease, which, complicated with some accident, resulted in an untimely death. He returned home a hopeless invalid, and his tedious illness was cheered by the affectionate tendance of her who had for so many years acted a mother's part towards him.

CHAPTER VII.

SCENES OF CLERICAL LIFE.

As has already been mentioned, Mr. Lewes and Marian went to Germany in 1854, dividing the year between Berlin, Munich, and Weimar. In the latter pleasant little Saxon city, on which the mighty influence of Goethe seemed still visibly resting, as the reflection of the sun lingers in the sky long after the sun himself has set, Lewes partly re-wrote his 'Life of Goethe.' Here must have been spent many delightful days, wandering in Goethe's track, exploring the beautiful neighbourhood, and enjoying some of the most cultivated society in Germany. Several articles on German life and literature, afterwards published in the *Westminster Review*, were probably written at this time. The translation of Spinoza's 'Ethics' by George Eliot was also executed in the same year. Mr. Lewes, alluding to it in 'Goethe's Life,' says, in a foot-note, "It may interest some readers to learn that Spinoza will ere long appear in English, edited by the writer of these lines." This was a delusive promise, since the translation has not yet made its appearance. But surely its publication would now be warmly welcomed.

The time, however, was approaching when George Eliot was at last to discover where her real mastery lay. And this is the way, as the story goes, that she discovered it. They had returned from the Continent and were settled again in London, both actively engaged in literature. But literature, unless in certain cases of triumphant popularity, is perhaps the worst paid of all work. Mr. Lewes and George Eliot were not too well off. The former, infinite in resources, having himself tried every form of literature in turn, could not fail to notice the matchless power of observation, and the memory matching it in power, of the future novelist. One day an idea struck him. "My dear," he said, "I think you could write a capital story." Shortly, afterwards there was some dinner engagement, but as he was preparing to go out, she said, "I won't go out this evening, and when you come in don't disturb me. I shall be very busy." And this was how the 'Scenes of Clerical Life' came first to be written! On being shown a portion of the first tale, 'Amos Barton,' Mr. Lewes was fairly amazed.

Stories are usually fabricated after the event; but, if not true, they often truly paint a situation. And the general testimony of friends seems to agree that it was Mr. Lewes who first incited the gifted woman, of whose great powers he was best able to form a judgment, to express herself in that species of literature which would afford the fullest scope to the creative and dramatic faculties which she so eminently possessed. Here, however, his influence ended. He helped to reveal George Eliot to herself, and after that there was little left for him to do. But this gift of stimulating another by sympathetic insight and critical appreciation is itself of priceless value. When Schiller died, Goethe said, "The half of my existence is gone

from me." A terrible word to utter for one so great.
But never again, he knew, would he meet with the
same complete comprehension, and, lacking that, his
genius itself seemed less his own than before.

There is an impression abroad that Mr. Lewes,
if anything, did some injury to George Eliot from
a literary point of view; that the nature of his
pursuits led her to adopt too technical and pedantic
a phraseology in her novels. But this idea is unjust
to both. In comparing her earliest with her latest
style, it is clear that from the first she was apt to cull
her illustrations from the physical sciences, thereby
showing how much these studies had become part of
herself. Indeed, she was far more liable to introduce
these scientific modes of expression than Mr. Lewes,
as may be easily seen by comparing his 'Life of
Goethe,' partly re-written in 1854, with some of her
essays of the same date. As to her matter, it is
curious how much of it was drawn from the earliest
sources of memory—from that life of her childhood
to which she may sometimes have turned yearningly
as to a long-lost Paradise. Most of her works might,
indeed, not inaptly be called 'Looking Backward.'
They are a half-pathetic, half-humorous, but entirely
tender revivification of the "days that are no more."
No one, however intimate, could really intermeddle
with the workings of a genius drawing its happiest
inspiration from the earliest experiences of its own
individual past.

Nothing is more characteristic of this obvious tendency than the first of the 'Scenes of Clerical Life,'
'The Sad Fortunes of the Rev. Amos Barton.' At
Chilvers Coton the curious in such matters may still
see the identical church where the incumbent of Shep-

perton used to preach sermons shrewdly compounded of High Church doctrines and Low Church evangelicalism, not forgetting to note "its little flight of steps with their wooden rail running up the outer wall, and leading to the school-children's gallery." There they may still see the little churchyard, though they may look in vain for the "slim black figure" of the Rev. Amos, "as it flits past the pale gravestones," in "the silver light that falls aslant on church and tomb." And among the tombs there is one, a handsome substantial monument, overshadowed by a yew-tree, on which there is this inscription :

HERE LIES,

WAITING THE SUMMONS OF THE ARCHANGEL'S TRUMPET,

ALL THAT WAS MORTAL OF

THE BELOVED WIFE OF THE

REV. JOHN GWYTHER, B.A.,

CURATE OF THIS PARISH,

NOV. 4TH, 1836,

AGED THIRTY-FOUR YEARS,

LEAVING A HUSBAND AND SEVEN CHILDREN.

This Emma Gwyther is none other than the beautiful Milly, the wife of Amos, so touchingly described by George Eliot, whose mother, Mrs. Evans, was her intimate friend. George Eliot would be in her teens when she heard the story of this sweet woman : heard the circumstantial details of her struggles to make the two ends of a ridiculously small income meet the yearly expenses : heard her mother, no doubt (in the words of Mrs. Hackit) blame her weak forbearance in tolerating the presence in her house of the luxurious and exacting countess, who, having ingratiated herself with the gullible Amos by her talk of the "livings" she would get him, gave much scandal in the neighbourhood : heard of the pathetic death-bed, when, worn by care and toil, the gentle life ebbed quietly away, leaving a life-long void in her husband's heart and home. All this was the talk of the neighbourhood when George Eliot was a girl ; and her extraordinary memory allowed nothing to escape.

On the completion of 'Amos Barton,' Mr. Lewes, who, as already mentioned, was a contributor to 'Maga.' sent the MS. to the editor, the late Mr. John Blackwood, as the work of an anonymous friend. This was in the autumn of 1856. The other scenes of 'Clerical Life' were then unwritten, but the editor was informed that the story submitted to his approval formed one of a series. Though his judgment was favourable, he begged to see some of the other tales before accepting this, freely making some criticisms on the plot and studies of character in 'Amos Barton.' This, however, disheartened the author, whose peculiar diffidence had only been overcome by Mr. Lewes's hearty commendation. When the editor had been made aware of the injurious effect of his objections, he hastened to efface it by accepting the tale without further delay. It appeared soon afterwards in *Blackwood's Magazine* for January 1857, where it occupied the first place. This story, by some considered as fine as anything the novelist ever wrote, came to an end in the next number. 'Mr. Gilfil's Love Story,' and 'Janet's Repentance' were written in quick succession, and the series was completed in November of the same year.

Although there was nothing sufficiently sensational in these 'Scenes' to arrest the attention of that great public which must be roused by something new and startling, literary judges were not slow to discern the powerful realism with which the author had drawn these uncompromising studies from life. After the appearance of 'Amos Barton,' Mr. Blackwood wrote to the anonymous author : "It is a long time since I have read anything so fresh, so humorous, and so touching. The style is capital, conveying so much in so few words." Soon afterwards he began another letter : "My dear Amos, I forget whether I told you or Lewes that I had shown part of the MS. to Thackeray. He was staying with me, and having been out at dinner, came in about eleven o'clock, when I had just finished reading it. I said to him, 'Do you know that I think I have lighted upon a new author, who is uncommonly like a first-class passenger.' I showed him a page or two, I think the passage where the curate returns home and Milly is first intro-duced. He would not pronounce whether it came up to my ideas, but remarked afterwards that he would have liked to have read more, which I thought a good sign."

Dickens, after the publication of the 'Scenes,' sent a letter to the unknown writer through the editor, warmly expressing the admiration he felt for them. But he was strongly of opinion from the first that they must have been written by a woman. In the meanwhile the tales were reprinted in a collected form, and they were so successful that the editor, writing to Mr. Lewes at the end of January 1858, when the book had hardly been out a month, was able to say, "George Eliot has fairly achieved a literary reputation among judges, and the public must follow, although it may take time." And in a letter to George Eliot herself, he wrote in February : "You will recollect, when we proposed to reprint, my impression was that the series had not lasted long enough in the magazine to give you a hold on the general public, although long enough to make your literary reputation. Unless in exceptional cases, a very long time often elapses between the two stages of reputation—the literary and the public. Your progress will be *sure*, if not so quick as we could wish."

While the sketches were being re-issued in book form, Messrs. Blackwood informed its author that they saw good cause for making a large increase in the forthcoming reprint, and their anticipations were fully justified by its success. All sorts of rumours were abroad as to the real author of these clerical tales. Misled by a hint, calculated to throw him off the real scent, Mr. Blackwood was at first under the impression that they were the work of a clergyman, and perhaps this may have been the origin of a belief which lingered till quite recently, that George Eliot was the daughter of a clergyman, a statement made by several of the leading daily papers after her death. Abandoning the idea of the clergyman, Mr. Blackwood next fixed upon a very different sort of person, to wit, Professor Owen, whom he suspected owing to the similarity of handwriting and the scientific knowledge so exceptional in a novelist. No less funny was the supposition held by others of Lord Lytton—who more than once hoaxed the public under a new literary disguise—having at last surpassed himself in the sterling excellence of these tales. Now that Bulwer has gone the way of all fashions, it seems incredible that the most obtuse and slow-witted of critics should have mistaken for a moment his high-flown sentimental style for the new author's terse, vigorous and simple prose.

It was impossible, however, for an author to remain a mere nameless abstraction. An appellation of some kind became an imperative necessity, and, during the passage of 'Mr. Gilfil's Love Story' through the press, the pseudonym of "George Eliot"—a name destined to become so justly renowned—was finally assumed.

The 'Scenes of Clerical Life' were to George Eliot's future works what a bold, spirited sketch is to a carefully elaborated picture. All the qualities that distinguished her genius may be discovered in this, her first essay in fiction. With all Miss Austen's matchless faculty for painting commonplace characters, George Eliot has that other nobler faculty of showing what tragedy, pathos, and humour may be lying in the experience of a human soul "that looks out through dull grey eyes, and that speaks in a voice of quite ordinary tones." While depicting some commonplace detail of every day life, she has the power to make her reader realise its close relation to the universal life. She never gives you the mere dry bones and fragments of existence as represented in some particular section of society, but always manages to keep before the mind the invisible links connecting it with the world at large. In 'Mr.' Gilfil's Love-Story' there is a passage as beautiful as any in her works, and fully illustrating this attitude of her mind. It is where Tina, finding herself deceived in Captain Wybrow, gives way to her passionate grief in solitude.

"While this poor little heart was being bruised with a weight too heavy for it, Nature was holding on her calm inexorable way, in unmoved and terrible beauty.

The stars were rushing in their eternal courses; the
tides swelled to the level of the last expectant weed;
the sun was making brilliant day to busy nations on
the other side of the swift earth. The stream of
human thought and deed was hurrying and broad-
ening onward. The astronomer was at his telescope;
the great ships were labouring over the waves; the
toiling eagerness of commerce, the fierce spirit of revolution, were only ebbing in brief rest; and sleepless
statesmen were dreading the possible crisis of the
morrow. What were our little Tina and her trouble
in this mighty torrent, rushing from one awful
unknown to another? Lighter than the smallest
centre of quivering life in the water-drop, hidden
and uncared for as the pulse of anguish in the breast
of the tiniest bird that has fluttered down to its nest
with the long-sought food, and has found the nest torn
and empty."

There is rather more incident in this story of Mr.
Gilfil than in either of the two other 'Scenes of
Clerical Life.' In 'Amos Barton' the narrative is of
the simplest, as has already been indicated; and
the elements from which 'Janet's Repentance' is
composed are as free from any complex entanglement
of plot. The author usually describes the most
ordinary circumstances of English life, but the powerful rendering of the human emotions which spring
from them takes a most vivid hold of the imagination: 'Mr. Gilfil's Love-Story,' however, seems a little
Italian romance dropped on English soil.

It is, in brief, the narration of how Sir Christopher
Cheverel and his wife, during their residence at Milan,
took pity on a little orphan girl, " whose large dark

H 2

cyes shone from out her queer little face like the
precious stones in a grotesque image carved in old
ivory." Caterina, or Tina as she is called, taken back
to 'Cheverel Manor, grew up under the care of the
Baronet's wife, to whom she became endeared by her
exceptional musical talent. Sir Christopher had no
children, but had chosen his nephew, Captain
Wybrow, for his heir, and planned a marriage
between him and Miss Assher, the handsome and
accomplished owner of a pretty estate. Another
marriage, on which he has equally set his heart, is
that between his ward Maynard Gilfil, an open-
eyed manly young fellow destined for the Church,
and the mellow-voiced, large-eyed Tina, for whom he
has long nursed an undeclared passion. But alas, for
the futility of human plans! Tina, to whom the
elegant Anthony Wybrow has been secretly pro-
fessing love, suffers tortures of jealousy when he
and Miss Assher, to whom he has dutifully become
engaged, come on a visit to Cheverel Manor. The
treacherous Captain, to lull the suspicions of his
betrothed, insinuates that poor Miss Sarti enter-
tains a hopeless passion for him, which puts the
poor girl, who gets an inkling of this double-dealing,
into a frenzy of indignation. In this state she possesses herself of a dagger, and as she is going to
meet the Captain by appointment, dreams of plunging
the weapon in the traitor's heart. But on reaching
the appointed spot, she beholds the false lover
stretched motionless on the ground already—having
suddenly died of heart disease. Tina's anguish is indescribable: she gives the alarm to the household,
but stung by remorse for a contemplated revenge
of which her tender-hearted nature was utterly in-

capable, she flies unperceived from the premises at night. Being searched for in vain, she is suspected of having committed suicide. After some days of almost unbearable suspense, news is brought that Tina is lying ill at the cottage of a former maid in the household. With reviving hopes her anxious lover rides to the farm, sees the half-stunned, un-happy girl, and, after a while, manages to remove her to his sister's house. She gradually recovers under Mrs. Heron's gentle tendance, and one day a child's accidental striking of a deep bass note on the harpsi-chord suddenly revives her old passionate delight in music. And 'the soul that was born anew to music was born anew to love.' After a while Tina agrees to become Mr. Gilfil's wife, who has been given the living at Shepperton, where a happy future seems in store for the Vicar. "But the delicate plant had been too deeply bruised, and in the struggle to put forth a blossom it died.

"Tina died, and Maynard Gilfil's love went with her into deep silence for evermore."

Besides this sympathy with the homeliest characters and situations, or, more properly speaking, springing from it, there already runs through these three tales the delicious vein of humour irradiating George Eliot's otherwise sombre pictures of life with sudden flashes of mirth as of sunlight trembling above dark waters. In this depth and richness of humour George Eliot not only takes precedence of all other distinguished women, but she stands among them without a rival. Hers is that thoughtful outlook on life, that infinite depth of observation which, taking note of the incon-sistencies and the blunders, the self-delusions and "fantastic pranks" of her fellow-men, finds the source

of laughter very near to tears ; never going out of her
way for the eccentric and peculiar in human nature,
seeing that human nature itself appears to her as the
epitome of all incongruity. It is this breadth of conception and unerringness of vision piercing through
the external and accidental to the core of man's
mixed nature which give certain of her creations
something of the life-like complexity of Shakespeare's.

Her power of rendering the idiom and manners of
peasants, artisans, and paupers, of calling up before us
the very gestures and phrases of parsons, country
practitioners, and other varieties of inhabitants of
our provincial towns and rural districts, already
manifests itself fully in these clerical stories. Here
we find such types as Mr. Dempster, the unscrupulous, brutal, drunken lawyer; Mr. Pilgrim, the
tall, heavy, rough-mannered, and spluttering doctor,
profusely addicted to bleeding and blistering his
patients; Mr. Gilfil, the eccentric · vicar, with a
tender love-story hidden beneath his rugged exterior; the large-hearted, unfortunate Janet, rescued
from moral ruin by Mr. Tryan, the ascetic evangelical clergyman, whose character, the author remarks,
might have been found sadly wanting in perfection by
feeble and fastidious minds, but, as she adds, "The
blessed work of helping the world forward happily
does not wait to be done by perfect men; and I
should imagine that neither Luther nor John Bunyan,
for example, would have satisfied the modern demand
for an ideal hero, who believes nothing but what is
true, feels nothing but what is exalted, and does
nothing but what is graceful. The real heroes of
God's making are quite different : they have their
natural heritage of love and conscience, which they

drew in with their mother's milk; they know one or two of those deep spiritual truths which are only to be won by long wrestling with their own sins and their own sorrows; they have earned faith and strength so far as they have done genuine work, but the rest is dry, barren theory, blank prejudice, vague hearsay."

George Eliot's early acquaintance with many types of the clerical character, and her sympathy with the religious life in all its manifestations, was never more fully shown than in these 'Scenes.' In 'Janet's Repentance' we already discover one of George Eliot's favourite psychological studies — the awakening of a morally mixed nature to a new, a spiritual life. This work of regeneration Mr. Tryan performs for Janet, Felix Holt for Esther, and Daniel Deronda for Gwendolen. Her protest against the application of too lofty a moral standard in judging of our fellow-creatures, her championship of the "mongrel, ungainly dogs who are nobody's pets," is another of the prominent qualities of her genius fully expressed in this firstling work, being, indeed, at the root of her humorous conception of life. One of the finest bits of humour in the present volume is the scene in 'Amos Barton,' which occurs at the workhouse, euphemistically called the "College." Mr. Barton, having just finished his address to the paupers, is thus accosted by Mr. Spratt, "a small-featured, small-statured man, with a remarkable power of language, mitigated by hesitation, who piqued himself on expressing unexceptionable sentiments in unexceptionable language on all occasions.

"'Mr. Barton, sir—aw—aw—excuse my trespassing on your time—aw—to beg that you will administer

a rebuke to this boy ; he is—aw—aw—most inveterate
in ill-behaviour during service-time.'

"The inveterate culprit was a boy of seven, vainly
contending against 'candles' at his nose by feeble
sniffing. But no sooner had Mr. Spratt uttered his
impeachment than Mrs. Fodge rushed forward,
and placed herself between Mr. Barton and the
accused.

"'That's *my* child, Muster Barton,' she exclaimed,
further manifesting her maternal instincts by applying
her apron to her offspring's nose. 'He's aly's a-findin'
faut wi' him, and a-poundin' him for nothin'. Let
him goo an' eat his roost goose as is a-smellin' up in
our noses while we're a-swallering them greasy broth,
an' let my boy alooan.'

"Mr. Spratt's small eyes flashed, and he was in
danger of uttering sentiments not unexceptionable
before the clergyman ; but Mr. Barton, foreseeing
that a prolongation of this episode would not
be to edification, said 'Silence!' in his severest
tones.

"'Let me hear no abuse. Your boy is not likely
to behave well, if you set him the example of being
saucy.' Then stooping down to Master Fodge, and
taking him by the shoulder, 'Do you like being
beaten?'

"'No—a.'

"'Then what a silly boy you are to be naughty.
If you were not naughty, you wouldn't be beaten.
But if you are naughty, God will be angry, as well
as Mr. Spratt ; and God can burn you for ever. That
will be worse than being beaten.'

"Master Fodge's countenance was neither affirma-
tive nor negative of this proposition.

"'But,' continued Mr. Barton, 'if you will be a good boy, God will love you, and you will grow up to be a good man. Now, let me hear next Thursday that you have been a good boy.'

"Master Fodge had no distinct vision of the benefit that would accrue to him from this change of courses."

CHAPTER VIII.

ADAM BEDE.

RARELY has a novelist come to his task with such a far-reaching culture, such an intellectual grasp, as George Eliot. We have seen her girlhood occupied with an extraordinary variety of studies; we have seen her plunged in abstruse metaphysical speculations; we have seen her translating some of the most laborious philosophical investigations of German thinkers; we have seen her again translating from the Latin the 'Ethics' of Spinoza; and, finally, we have seen her attracting, and attracted by, some of the leaders in science, philosophy, and literature.

Compared with such qualifications who among novelists could compete? What could a Dickens, or a Thackeray himself, throw into the opposing scale? Lewes, indeed, was a match for her in variety of attainments, but he had made several attempts at fiction, and the attempts had proved failures. When at last, in the maturity of her powers, George Eliot produced 'Adam Bede,' she produced a novel in which the amplest results of knowledge and meditation were so happily blended with instinctive insight into life and character, and the rarest dramatic imagination, as to stamp it immediately as one of the great triumphs and masterpieces in the world of fiction.

It is worth noticing that in 'Adam Bede' George Eliot fulfils to the utmost the demands which she had been theoretically advocating in her essays. In some of these she had not only eloquently enforced the importance of a truthful adherence to nature, but had pointed out how the artist is thus in the very vanguard of social and political reforms; as in familiarising the imagination with the real condition of the people, he did much towards creating that sympathy with their wants, their trials, and their sufferings, which would eventually effect external changes in harmony with this better understanding. Such had been her teaching. And in Dickens she had recognised the one great novelist who, in certain respects, had painted the lower orders with unerring truthfulness. His " Oliver Twists," his " Nancys," his " Joes," were terrible and pathetic pictures of the forlorn outcasts haunting our London streets. And if, as George Eliot says, Dickens had been able to "give us their psychological character, their conception of life and their emotions, with the same truth as their idiom and manners, his books would be the greatest contribution Art has ever made to the awakening of social sympathies." Now George Eliot absolutely does what Dickens aimed at doing. She not merely seizes the outward and accidental traits of her characters : she pierces with unerring vision to the very core of their nature, and enables us to realise the peculiarly subtle relations between character and circumstance. Her primary object is to excite our sympathy with the most ordinary aspects of human life, with the people that one may meet any day in the fields, the workshops, and the homes of England. Her most vivid creations are not exceptional beings, not men or women pre-eminently conspicuous for sublime heroism of character or magnificent mental endowments, but work-a-day folk,

> " Not too fine or good
> For human nature's daily food."

To this conscientious fidelity of observation and anxious endeavour to report the truth and nothing but the truth, as of a witness in a court of justice, are owing that life-like vividness with which the scenery and people in 'Adam Bede' seem projected on the reader's imagination. The story, indeed, is so intensely realistic as to have given rise to the idea that it is entirely founded on fact. That there is such a substratum is hardly a matter of doubt, and there have been various publications all tending to prove that the chief characters in 'Adam Bede' were not only very faithful copies of living people, but of people closely connected with its author. To some extent this is incontrovertible. But, on the other hand, there is a likelihood of the fictitious events having in their turn been grafted on to actual personages and occurrences, till the whole has become so fused together as to lead some persons to the firm conviction that Dinah Morris is absolutely identical with Mrs. Elizabeth Evans, the Derbyshire Methodist. Such a supposition would help to reconcile the conflicting statements respectively made by the great novelist and the writers of two curious little books entitled 'Seth Bede, the Methody, his Life and Labours,' chiefly written by

himself, and 'George Eliot in Derbyshire,' by Guy
Roslyn.

From these brochures one gathers that Hayslope,
where the rustic drama of 'Adam Bede' unfolds
itself, is the village of Ellaston, not far from Ashbourne
in Staffordshire. This village is so little altered
that the traveller may still see the sign-board of the
"Donnithorne Arms," and the red brick hall, only
with windows no longer unpatched. Samuel, William,
and Robert Evans (the father of the novelist) were
born in this place, and began life as carpenters, as
their father before them. Samuel Evans became a
zealous Methodist, and was rather laughed at by his
family in consequence, for he says, "My elder
brothers often tried to tease me; they entertained
High Church principles. They told me what great
blunders I made in preaching and prayer; that I had
more zeal than knowledge." In this, as in other
respects, he is the prototype of Seth, as Adam resembles Robert Evans, one of the more secular elder
brothers, only that in real life it was Samuel who
married Elizabeth, the Dinah Morris of fiction.

Much has been written about this Elizabeth Evans
(the aunt of George Eliot, already spoken of): indeed,
her life was one of such rare devotion to an ideal
cause, that even such imperfect fragments of it as
have been committed to writing by herself or her
friends are of considerable interest. Elizabeth was
born at Newbold in Leicestershire, and left her
father's house when little more than fourteen years
old. She joined the Methodists in 1797, after which
she had entirely done with the pleasures of the world
and all her old companions. "I saw it my duty,"
she says, "to leave off all my superfluities of dress,

hence I pulled off all my bunches, cut off my curls, left off my lace, and in this I found an unspeakable pleasure. I saw I could make a better use of my time and money than to follow the fashions of a vain world." While still a beautiful young girl, attired in a quaker dress and bonnet, she used to walk across those bleak Derbyshire hills which look so strangely mournful in their treeless nudity, with their bare stone fences grey against a greyer sky. Here she trudged from village to village gathering the poor about her, and pouring forth words of such earnest conviction that, as she says, "Many were brought to the Lord." The points of resemblance between her career and that of Dinah Morris cannot fail to strike the reader, even their phraseology being often singularly alike, as when Mrs. Evans writes in the short account of what she calls her "unprofitable life:" "I saw it my duty to be wholly devoted to God, and to be set apart for the Master's use;" while Dinah says: "My life is too short, and God's work is too great for me to think of making a home for myself in this world." It must be borne in mind, however, that these similarities of expression are natural enough when one considers that Dinah is a type of the same old-fashioned kind of Methodism to which Mrs. Evans belonged. What is perhaps stranger is, that the account given by George Eliot of her various meetings with her aunt, Mrs. Elizabeth Evans, should differ considerably from what the latter herself remembered or has stated about them. Shortly after the appearance of 'Adam Bede,' attention had been publicly called to the identity of the heroine of fiction with the Methodist preacher. This conviction was so strong in Wirksworth, that a number of friends placed a

memorial tablet in the Methodist chapel at Wirksworth with the following inscription :—

ERECTED BY GRATEFUL FRIENDS,

𝔍𝔫 𝔐𝔢𝔪𝔬𝔯𝔂 𝔬𝔣

MRS. ELIZABETH EVANS,

(KNOWN TO THE WORLD AS "DINAH BEDE")

WHO DURING MANY YEARS PROCLAIMED ALIKE IN THE
OPEN AIR, THE SANCTUARY, AND FROM HOUSE
TO HOUSE,

THE LOVE OF CHRIST:

SHE DIED IN THE LORD, MAY 9TH, 1849; AGED 74 YEARS.

In order to give a correct notion of the amount of
truth in her novel, George Eliot wrote in the following
terms to her friend Miss Hennell on the 7th of
October, 1859: "I should like, while the subject is
vividly present with me, to tell you more exactly
than I have ever yet done, *what* I knew of my aunt,
Elizabeth Evans. My father, you know, lived in
Warwickshire all my life with him, having finally left
Staffordshire first, and then Derbyshire, six or seven
years before he married my mother. There was
hardly any intercourse between my father's family,
resident in Derbyshire and Staffordshire, and our
family—few and far between visits of (to my childish
feeling) strange uncles and aunts and cousins from
my father's far-off native county, and once a journey
of my own, as a little child, with my father and
mother, to see my uncle William (a rich builder) in
Staffordshire—but *not* my uncle and aunt Samuel, so
far as I can recall the dim outline of things—are what
I remember of northerly relatives in my childhood.

"But when I was seventeen or more—after my

sister was married, and I was mistress of the house—
my father took a journey into Derbyshire, in which,
visiting my uncle and aunt Samuel, who were very
poor, and lived in a humble cottage at Wirksworth,
he found my aunt in a very delicate state of health
after a serious illness, and, to do her bodily good, he
persuaded her to return with him, telling her that *I*
should be very, very happy to have her with me for a
few weeks. I was then strongly under the influence
of evangelical belief, and earnestly endeavouring to
shape this anomalous English-Christian life of ours
into some consistency with the spirit and simple
verbal tenor of the New Testament. I *was* delighted
to see my aunt. Although I had only heard her
spoken of as a strange person, given to a fanatical
vehemence of exhortation in private as well as public,
I believed that I should find sympathy between us.
She was then an old woman—above sixty—and, I
believe, had for a good many years given up preaching. A tiny little woman, with bright, small dark
eyes, and hair that had been black, I imagine, but
was now grey—a pretty woman in her youth, but of
a totally different physical type from Dinah. The difference—as you will believe—was not *simply* physical ;
no difference is. She was a woman of strong natural
excitability, which I know, from the description I
have heard my father and half-sister give, prevented
her from the exercise of discretion under the promptings of her zeal. But this vehemence was now subdued by age and sickness ; she was very gentle and
quiet in her manners, very loving, and (what she must
have been from the very first), a truly religious soul,
in whom the love of God and love of man were fused
together. There was nothing rightly distinctive in

her religious conversation. I had had much intercourse with pious dissenters before; the only freshness I found in her talk came from the fact that she
had been the greater part of her life a Wesleyan, and
though *she left the society when women were no longer
allowed to preach,* and joined the New Wesleyans, she
retained the character of thought that belongs to the
genuine old Wesleyan. I had never talked with a
Wesleyan before, and we used to have little debates
about predestination, for I was then a strong Calvinist.
Here her superiority came out, and I remember now,
with loving admiration, one thing which at the time I
disapproved; it was not strictly a consequence of her
Arminian belief, and at first sight might seem opposed
to it, yet it came from the spirit of love which clings
to the bad logic of Arminianism. When my uncle
came to fetch her, after she had been with us a fort-
night or three weeks, he was speaking of a deceased
minister once greatly respected, who, from the action
of trouble upon him, had taken to small tippling,
though otherwise not culpable. 'But I hope the good
man's in heaven for all that,' said my uncle. 'Oh
yes,' said my aunt, with a deep inward groan of
joyful conviction, 'Mr. A.'s in heaven, that's sure.'
This was at the time an offence to my stern, ascetic,
hard views—how beautiful it is to me now!

"As to my aunt's conversation, it is a fact that the
only two things of any interest I remember in our
lonely sittings and walks are her telling me one sunny
afternoon how she had, with another pious woman,
visited an unhappy girl in prison, stayed with her all
night, and gone with her to execution; and one or
two accounts of supposed miracles in which she
believed, among the rest, *the face with the crown of*

thorns seen in the glass. In her account of the prison scenes I remember no word she uttered; I only remember her tone and manner, and the deep feeling I had under the recital. Of the girl she knew nothing, I believe, or told me nothing, but that she was a common, coarse girl, convicted of child-murder. The incident lay in my mind for years on years, as a dead germ, apparently, till time had made my mind a nidus in which it could fructify; it then turned out to be the germ of 'Adam Bede.'

"I saw my aunt twice after this. Once I spent a day and night with my father in the Wirksworth cottage, sleeping with my aunt, I remember. Our interview was less interesting than in the former time; I think I was less simply devoted to religious ideas. And once again she came with my uncle to see me, when father and I were living at Foleshill; *then* there was some pain, for I had given up the form of Christian belief, and was in a crude state of free-thinking. She stayed about three or four days, I think. This is all I remember distinctly, as matter I could write down, of my dear aunt, whom I really loved. You see how she suggested 'Dinah;' but it is not possible you should see, as I do, how entirely her individuality differed from 'Dinah's.' How curious it seems to me that people should think 'Dinah's' sermon, prayers, and speeches were *copied*, when they were written with hot tears as they surged up in my own mind!

"As to my indebtedness to facts of local and personal history of a small kind connected with Staffordshire and Derbyshire, you may imagine of what kind that is, when I tell you that I never remained in either of those counties more than a few days together, and of only two such visits have I more than a shadowy, interrupted recollection. The details which I know as facts, and have made use of for my picture, were gathered from such imperfect allusion and narrative as I heard from my father in his occasional talk about old times.

"As to my aunt's children or grandchildren saying, if they *did* say, that 'Dinah' is a good portrait of my aunt, that is simply the vague, easily-satisfied notion imperfectly-instructed people always have of portraits. It is not surprising that simple men and women, without pretension to enlightened discrimination, should think a generic resemblance constitutes a portrait, when we see the great public, so accustomed to be delighted with *mis*-representations of life and character, which they accept as representations, that they are scandalised when art makes a nearer approach to truth.

"Perhaps I am doing a superfluous thing in writing all this to you, but I am prompted to do it by the feeling that in future years 'Adam Bede,' and all that concerns it, may have become a dim portion of the past, and that I may not be able to recall so much of the truth as I have now told you."

Nothing could prove more conclusively how powerful was the impression which 'Adam Bede' created than this controversy concerning the amount of truth which its characters contained. But, as hinted before, it seems very likely that some of the doings and sayings of the fictitious personages should have been attributed, almost unconsciously, to the real people whom they resembled. How quick is the popular imagination in effecting these transformations came only quite recently under my notice, when some English tra-

vellers, while visiting Château d'If, were taken by
the guide in perfect good faith to see the actual dun-
geon where Monte Christo was imprisoned! Similarly,
one would think, that the moving sermon preached
by Dinah on the Green at Hayslope had been
afterwards erroneously ascribed to Mrs. Elizabeth
Evans. But an account recently published in the
Century Magazine by one who had long known the
Evanses of Wirksworth, seems irreconcilable with such
a supposition. According to this writer it would
appear that besides the visits to her aunt at Wirksworth, of which George Eliot speaks in the letter just
quoted, there was one other of which no mention
is made. This visit, which she paid her cousin, Mr.
Samuel Evans, occurred in 1842, when she remained
a week at his house in Wirksworth. The aunt and
niece were in the habit of seeing each other every
day for several hours at this time. They usually met
at the house of one of the married daughters of Mrs.
Elizabeth Evans, holding long conversations while
sitting by themselves in the parlour. "These secret
conversations," says the writer of the article, "excited
some curiosity in the family, and one day one of the
daughters said, 'Mother, I can't think what thee and
Mary Ann have got to talk about so much.' To
which Mrs. Evans replied: 'Well, my dear, I don't
know what she wants, but she gets me to tell her all
about my life and my religious experience, and she
puts it all down in a little book. I can't make out
what she wants it for.'" After her departure, Mrs.
Evans is reported to have said to her daughter, "Oh
dear, Mary Ann has got one thing I did not mean her
to take away, and that is the notes of the first sermon
I preached at Ellaston Green." According to the

same authority, Marian Evans took notes of everything people said in her hearing : no matter who was
speaking, down it went into the note-book, which
seemed never out of her hand ; and these notes she
is said to have transcribed every night before going
to bed. Yet this habit was foreign to her whole
character, and the friends who knew her most intimately in youth and later life never remember seeing
her resort to such a practice. Be that as it may,
there can be no doubt that the novelist very freely
used many of the circumstances connected with her
aunt's remarkable career. How closely she adhered
to nature is shown by the fact that in Mrs. Poyser
and Bartle Massey she retained the actual names of
the characters portrayed, as they happened to be both
dead. Bartle Massey, the village cynic, had been
the schoolmaster of her father, Robert Evans. How
accurately the latter, together with all his surroundings, was described is shown by the following anecdote.
On its first appearance 'Adam Bede' was read aloud
to an old man, an intimate associate of Robert
Evans in his Staffordshire days. This man knew
nothing concerning either author or subject before-
hand, and his astonishment was boundless on recognising so many friends and incidents of his own
youth portrayed with unerring fidelity. He sat up
half the night listening to the story in breathless
excitement, now and then slapping his knee as he
exclaimed, "That's Robert, that's Robert to the life."
Although Wirksworth is not the locality described
in 'Adam Bede,' it contains features recalling that
quaint little market-town, where over the door of one
of the old-fashioned houses may be read the name
made illustrious by the inimitable Mrs. Poyser. In

the neighbourhood, too, are "Arkwright's mills there at Cromford," casually alluded to by Adam Bede; and should the tourist happen to enter one of the cottages of grey stone, with blue-washed door and window-frames, he may still alight on specimens of Methodism, as devout as Seth Bede, eloquently expounding the latest political event by some prophecy of Daniel or Ezekiel. In short, one breathes the atmosphere in which such characters as Dinah and Seth actually lived and had their being. This uncompromising Realism, so far from detracting, only enhances the genius of this powerful novel. A thousand writers might have got hold of these identical materials: a George Eliot alone could have cast these materials into the mould of 'Adam Bede.' Let any one glance at the account of their religious experiences, as given by Elizabeth or Samuel Evans, and he will realise all the more strongly how great was the genius of her who transfused these rambling, commonplace effusions into such an artistic whole. I have entered so minutely into this question of the likeness between the actual characters and those in the novel purely on account of the biographical interest attaching to it. In judging of 'Adam Bede' as a work of art these facts possess next to no importance. If we could trace the characters in any one of Shakespeare's plays to human beings actually connected with the poet, we should consider such a discovery immensely valuable as throwing new light on his own life, though it would hardly affect our critical estimate of the drama itself.

So much has been said already about the characters in 'Adam Bede' in connection with the real people they resemble, that little need be added here about them. Dinah Morris—the youthful preacher, whose eloquence is but the natural, almost involuntary manifestation in words, of a beautiful soul; whose spring of love is so abundant that it overflows the narrow limits of private affection, and blesses multitudes of toiling, suffering men and women with its wealth of pity, hope, and sympathy—was a new creation in the world of fiction. Some writer has pointed out a certain analogy between the sweet Derbyshire Methodist and the gentle pietist whose confessions form a very curious chapter of 'Wilhelm Meister.' But the two characters are too dissimilar for comparison. The German heroine is a dreamy, passive, introspective nature, feeling much but doing little; whereas the English preacher does not inquire too curiously into the mysteries of her faith, but moved by the spirit of its teaching goes about actively, participating in the lives of others by her rousing words and her acts of charity. Only a woman would or could have described just such a woman as this: a woman whose heart is centred in an impersonal ideal instead of in any individual object of love; whereas a man's heroine always has her existence rooted in some personal affection or passion, whether for parent or lover, child or husband. This makes Dinah less romantically interesting than Hetty Sorrel, the beautiful, kittenlike, self-involved creature with whom she is so happily contrasted. George Eliot never drew a more living figure than this of Hetty, hiding such a hard little heart under that soft dimpling beauty of hers. Again, I think that only a woman would have depicted just such a Hetty as this. The personal charms of this young girl are drawn in words that have the glow of life itself; yet while intensely conscious of her beauty, we are kept aware all the time that, to use one of the famous Mrs. Poyser's epigrammatic sayings, Hetty is "no better nor a cherry wi' a hard stone inside it." George Eliot is never dazzled or led away by her own bewitching creation as a man would have been. There is a certain pitilessness in her analysis of Hetty's shallow, frivolous little soul, almost as if she were saying—See here, what stuff this beauty which you adore is made of in reality! To quote her own subtle, far-reaching interpretation of beauty: "Hetty's face had a language that transcended her feelings. There are faces which nature charges with a meaning and pathos not be-longing to the simple human soul that flutters beneath them, but speaking the joys and sorrows of foregone generations; eyes that tell of deep love which doubt-less has been and is somewhere, but not paired with these eyes, perhaps paired with pale eyes that can say nothing, just as a national language may be instinct with poetry unfelt by the lips that use it."

The sensation created by 'Adam Bede' was shown in other ways besides the claim of some to have dis-covered the original characters of this striking novel. The curiosity of the public was naturally much exer-cised as to who the unknown author could possibly be, who had so suddenly leaped into fame. And now there comes on the scene an individual who does not claim to be the living model of one of the characters portrayed, but to be the author of the book himself. And the name of this person was Liggins!

While the 'Scenes of Clerical Life' were yet appear-ing in *Blackwood's Magazine* the inhabitants of Nun-eaton and its neighbourhood were considerably per-plexed and excited to find well-known places and

persons touched off to the life. In Amos Barton
they recognised the incumbent of Coton Church, in
Mr. Pilgrim a medical man familiar to every child
in the town, and indeed in every one of the characters
an equally unmistakable portrait. Clearly no one
but a fellow-townsman could have hit off these
wonderful likenesses. Literary talent not being too
abundant, their choice of an author was limited.
The only man who by any stretch of imagination
seemed to have the making of a man of letters in him
was this above-mentioned Liggins. To have studied
at Cambridge, gallantly run through a fortune, and be
in very needy circumstances, were exactly the qualifications to be expected in a man of genius. Further
evidence seeming unnecessary, the real authorship of
the 'Scenes' was now revealed in an Isle of Man
paper. At first the reputed author gently denied the
impeachment, but on the appearance of 'Adam Bede'
he succumbed to the temptation. To be fêted at
dinner parties as a successful author, and to have a
subscription set on foot by enthusiastic lady-admirers
and fellow-townsmen, in whose eyes he was a sadly
unrequited genius, proved irresistible. A local clergyman even wrote to the *Times* stating Liggins to be
the real surname of "George Eliot!" The latter
wrote, of course, denying the statement, and challeng-
ing the pretender to produce some specimen of his
writing in the style of 'Adam Bede.' But the confidence of the Nuneaton public in their hero Liggins
was not to be so easily shaken. Two dissenting
ministers from Coventry went over to Attleborough
to call upon the "great author," and to find out if he
really did write 'Adam Bede.' Liggins evaded their
questions, indirectly admitting that he did ; but when

they asked him point blank, " Liggins, tell us, *did* you write 'Adam Bede'?" he said, "If I didn't, the devil did!" and that was all they could get out of him. Another clergyman was much less sceptical, assuring every one that he was positive as to Liggins being the author, as he had seen the MS. of 'Adam Bede' in his hands. To this day there lives in the Isle of Man a certain venerable old gentleman who has never lost his faith in Liggins, but, when George Eliot is mentioned, gravely shakes his head, implying that there is more in the name than meets the eye of the superficial observer. But a heavy retribution befell the poor pseudo-author at last, for when his false pretences to favour were fully manifest he fell into utter neglect and poverty, ending his days in the workhouse.

This foolish misrepresentation hastened the disclosure of George Eliot's real personality and name, which occurred on the publication of the 'Mill on the Floss.' Shortly before that, Mr. Blackwood, who had long entertained the wish to know the author of the 'Scenes of Clerical Life' and of 'Adam Bede,' was invited by Lewes to meet him at last. No one was present at the dinner-table besides Mr. Lewes, Marian, and Mr. Blackwood himself. The dinner was an extremely pleasant one, but when it was over, the guest could not help expressing his regret that George Eliot himself should not have been present. "Here he is," said Lewes, introducing the quiet, low-spoken lady who had presided at table, not without enjoyment at the sensation he produced as the astonished publisher shook hands with his contributor.

CHAPTER IX.

THE MILL ON THE FLOSS.

WHILE the public had been trying to discover who the mysterious George Eliot could possibly be, one person there was who immediately penetrated the disguise, and felt positive as to the identity of the author. On reading the 'Scenes,' and especially 'Adam Bede,' he was convinced that no one but a member of his own family could have written these stories. He recognised incidents, touches, a saying here or there, just the things that no one outside his own home could by any chance have come upon. But George Eliot's brother kept this discovery closely locked within his own breast. He trembled lest any one else should discover the secret, fearing the outcry of neighbours who might not always feel that the author had represented them in colours sufficiently flattering.

When the 'Mill on the Floss' appeared, however, the veil was lifted, and people heard that George Eliot had once been a Miss Marian Evans, who came from the neighbourhood of Nuneaton in Warwickshire. To her brother Isaac alone this was no news, as he had detected his sister in the first of the 'Scenes.' The child-life of Tom and Maggie Tulliver was in many respects an autobiography; and no biographer can ever hope to describe the early history of George

Eliot as she herself has done in the 'Mill on the
Floss.' How many joys and griefs of those happy careless days must have been recalled to her brother—those
days when little Mary Ann had sat poring over Daniel
Defoe's 'History of the Devil'—or sought refuge in
the attic at Griff house, after a quarrel with him :
"This attic was Maggie's favourite retreat on a wet day,
when the weather was not too cold ; here she fretted
out all her ill-humours, and talked aloud to the worm-
eaten floors and the worm-eaten shelves, and the dark
rafters festooned with cobwebs ; and here she kept a
Fetish which she punished for all her misfortunes.
This was the trunk of a large wooden doll, which once
stared with the roundest of eyes above the reddest of
cheeks, but was now entirely defaced by a long career
of vicarious suffering. Three nails driven into the
head commemorated as many crises in Maggie's nine
years of earthly struggle, that luxury of vengeance
having been suggested to her by the picture of Jael
destroying Sisera in the old Bible."

Again, at some fields' distance from their old home
there had been a " Round Pool " called "The Moat,"
" almost a perfect round, framed in with willows and
tall reeds, so that the water was only to be seen when
you got close to the brink." This was a favourite
resort of Isaac and Mary Ann, as also of Tom and
his sister when they went fishing together, and
" Maggie thought it probable that the small fish would
come to her hook and the large ones to Tom's." The
" Red Deeps," too, where Maggie loved to walk in
June, when the " dog-roses were in their glory," and
where she lived through many phases of her shifting
inner life was in the same vicinity, and at one time a
beloved haunt of the future novelist.

But although some of the spots mentioned in the
'Mill on the Floss' have been easily identified as
connected with George Eliot's early home, the scenery
of that novel is mainly laid in Lincolnshire. St. Oggs,
with "its red-fluted roofs and broad warehouse gables,"
is the ancient town of Gainsborough. The Floss is a
tidal river like the Trent, and in each case the springtide, rushing up the river with its terrific wave and
flooding the land for miles round, is known as the
Eagre, a name not a little descriptive of the thing
itself.

The 'Mill on the Floss' (a title adopted by the
author at the suggestion of Mr. Blackwood in preference to 'Sister Maggie') is the most poetical of
George Eliot's novels. The great Floss, hurrying
between green pastures to the sea, gives a unity
of its own to this story, which opens to the roar of
waters, the weltering waters which accompany it at
the close. It forms the elemental background which
rounds the little lives of the ill-starred family group
nurtured on its banks. The childhood of Tom and
Maggie Tulliver is inextricably blended with this
swift river, the traditions of which have been to them
as fairy tales; its haunting presence is more or less
with them throughout their chequered existence; and
when pride and passion, when shame and sorrow have
divided the brother and sister, pursued as by some
tragic fate, the Floss seems to rise in sympathy, and
submerges them in its mighty waters to unite them
once more "in an embrace never to be parted." It
cannot fail to strike the reader that in almost every
one of George Eliot's novels there occurs a death by
drowning: as in the instance of Thias Bede, of
Dunstan Cass, of Henleigh Grandcourt, and nearly in

that of Tito. This may be accounted for by the fact that as a child the novelist became acquainted with the sudden death of a near relative who had accidentally fallen into a stream : an incident which sunk deeply into her retentive mind.

Fate plays a very conspicuous part in this as in most of George Eliot's novels. But it is not the Fate of the Greeks, it is not a power that affects human existence from without : it rather lies at the root of it, more or less shaping that existence according to obscure inherited tendencies, and in the collision between character and circumstance, between passion and law, potent only in proportion as the individual finally issues conquered or a conqueror from the struggle of life. This action of character on circumstance, and of circumstance on character is an ever-recurring *motif* with George Eliot. We constantly see adverse circumstances modifying and moulding the lives of the actors in her stories. She has hardly, if ever, therefore, drawn a hero or heroine, for these, instead of yielding, make circumstances yield to them. Dorothea and Lydgate in abandoning their striving after the highest kind of life ; Tito in invariably yielding to the most pleasurable prompting of the moment ; Gwendolen in being mainly influenced by circumstances acting on her, without her reacting on them, are all types of this kind.

Maggie belongs, on the whole, to the same type. She, too, is what Goethe calls a problematic nature, a nature which, along with vast possibilities and lofty aspirations, lacks a certain fixity of purpose, and drifting helplessly from one extreme to another, is shattered almost as soon as it has put out of port. In Maggie's case this evil springs from the very fulness of her nature ; from the acuteness of an imagination which the many-sidedness of life attracts by turns in the most opposite directions. Tom, on the other hand, with his narrow practical understanding, entirely concentrated on the business in hand, swerves neither to right nor left, because he may be said to resemble a horse with blinkers, in that he sees only the road straight ahead. Maggie, with all her palpable weaknesses and startling inconsistencies, is the most adorable of George Eliot's women. In all poetry and fiction there is no child more delicious than the "little wench" with her loving heart and dreamy ways, her rash impulses and wild regrets, her fine susceptibilities and fiery jets of temper—in a word, her singularly fresh and vital nature. The same charm pervades every phase of her life. In her case the child, if I may so far modify Wordsworth's famous saying, is eminently the mother of the woman.

Profoundly affectionate by nature, and sympathising as she does with her father in his calamity, she cannot help rebelling at the sordid narrowness of her daily life, passionately craving for a wider field wherein to develop her inborn faculties. In this state of yearning and wild unrest, her accidental reading of Thomas à Kempis forms a crisis in her life, by bringing about a spiritual awakening in which Christianity, for the first time, becomes a living truth to her. Intense as she is, Maggie now throws all the ardour of her nature into renunciation and self-conquest. She seeks her highest satisfaction in abnegation of all personal desire, and in entire devotion to others. In her young asceticism she relinquishes a world of which she is ignorant, stifling every impulse, however innocent, that seems opposed to her new faith.

But Maggie has more actual affinity with poets and artists than with saints and martyrs. Her soul thrills like a finely-touched instrument to the beauty of the world around her, and though she doubts whether there may not even be a sinfulness in the indulgence of this enjoyment, yet the summer flowers and the summer sunshine put her scruples to flight. And then, when, through the intervention of Philip Wakem, the enchantments of romance and poetry are brought within her reach, the glory of the world again lays hold of her imagination, and a fresh conflict is begun in her soul. Thus she drifts from one state into another most opposed to it, and to an outside observer, such as Tom, her abrupt transitions are a sign that she is utterly wanting in moral stamina.

Not only Tom, but many eminent critics, who have descanted with fond partiality on Maggie's early life, seem to be shocked by that part of her story in which she allows herself to fall passionately in love with such an ordinary specimen of manhood as Stephen Guest. The author has even been accused of violating the truth of Nature, inasmuch as such a high-minded woman as Maggie could never have inclined to so vulgar, so commonplace a man as her lover. Others, while not questioning the truth of the character, find fault with the poor heroine herself, whom they pronounce an ineffective nature revealing its innate unsoundness by the crowning error of an abject passion for so poor a creature as the dandy of St. Oggs. This contention only proves the singular vitality of the character itself, and nothing is more psychologically true in George Eliot's studies of character than this love of the high-souled heroine for a man who has no corresponding

fineness of fibre in his nature, his attraction lying
entirely in the magnetism of mutual passion. This
vitality places Maggie Tulliver by the side of the
Juliets, the Mignons, the Consuelos, the Becky Sharps
and other airy inheritors of immortality. It is curious
that Mr. Swinburne, in view of such a character as
this, or, indeed, bearing in mind a Silas Marner, a
Dolly Winthrop, a Tito, and other intrinsically living
reproductions of human nature, should describe George
Eliot's as intellectually constructed characters in contrast to Charlotte Brontë's creations, the former,
according to him, being the result of intellect, the
latter of genius.   If ever character came simply
dropped out of the mould of Nature it is that
of Maggie.   His assumption, that the 'Mill on the
Floss' can in any sense have been suggested by, or
partially based upon, Mrs. Gaskell's story of 'The
Moorland Cottage,' seems equally baseless.   There is
certainly the identity of name in the heroines, and
some resemblance of situation as regards portions of
the story, but both the name and the situation are
sufficiently common not to excite astonishment at
such a coincidence.   Had George Eliot really known
of this tale—a tale feebly executed at the best—she
would obviously have altered the name so as not to
make her obligation too patent to the world.   As it
is, she was not a little astonished and even indignant,
on accidentally seeing this opinion stated in some
review, and positively denied ever having seen the
story in question.

Indeed when one knows how this story grew out of
her own experience, how its earlier portions especially
are a record of her own and her brother's childhood—
how even Mrs. Glegg and Mrs. Pullet were only

K

too faithfully done from the aunts of real life, one
need not go far afield to seek for its origin. Every
author usually writes one book, which he might more
or less justly entitle 'My Confessions,' into which he
pours an intimate part of his life under a thin disguise
of fiction, a book invariably exciting a unique kind
of interest in the reader be he conscious or not of the
presence of this autobiographical element. Fielding's
'Amelia,' Thackeray's 'Pendennis,' Dickens's 'David
Copperfield,' Charlotte Brontë's 'Villette,' are cases in
point. The 'Mill on the Floss' is a work of similar
nature. Maggie Tulliver is George Eliot herself, but
only one side, one portion, one phase of George
Eliot's many-sided, vastly complex nature.   It is
George Eliot's inner life in childhood and youth as it
appeared to her own consciousness. We recognise in
it her mental acuteness, her clinging affectionateness,
her ambition, her outlook beyond the present, her religious and moral preoccupations, even her genius is not
so much omitted as left in an undeveloped, rudimen-
tary state ; while her make-believe stories, her thirst
for knowledge, her spiritual wrestlings, and the passionate response of her soul to high thinking, noble
music, and the beautiful in all its forms, show that
the making of genius was there in germ. Much in
the same manner Goethe was fond of partitioning
his nature, and of giving only the weaker side to his
fictitious representatives.   Conscious in himself of
fluctuations of purpose which he only got the better
of by his indomitable will, he usually endowed these
characters with his more impulsive, pliant self, as
manifested in Werther, in Tasso, in Edward of
the 'Elective Affinities.'   In this sense also Maggie
Tulliver resembles George Eliot. She is her poten-

tial self, such as she might have been had there not been counterbalancing tendencies of unusual force, sufficient to hold in check all erratic impulses contrary to the main direction of her life.

While tempted to dwell largely on Maggie Tulliver, the central figure of 'The Mill on the Floss,' it would be very unfair to slur over the other admirably drawn characters of this novel. Her brother Tom, already repeatedly alluded to, is in every sense the counterpart of "Sister Maggie." Hard and narrow-minded he was from a boy, " particularly clear and positive on one point, namely, that he would punish everybody who deserved it : why, he wouldn't have minded being punished himself, if he deserved it ; but, then, he never *did* deserve it." This strikes the key-note of a character whose stern inflexibility, combined with much practical insight and dogged persistence of effort, is at the same time dignified by a high, if somewhat narrow, sense of family honour. Conventional respectability, in fact, is Tom Tulliver's religion. He is not in any sense bad, or mean, or sordid ; he is only so circumscribed in his perceptive faculties, that he has no standard by which to measure thoughts or feelings that transcend his own very limited conception of life.

Both by his good and his bad qualities, by his excellencies and his negations, Tom Tulliver proves himself what he is—a genuine sprig of the Dodson family, a chip of the old block! And the Dodson sisters are, in their way, among the most amazingly living portraitures that George Eliot ever achieved. Realism in art can go no further in this direction. These women, if present in the flesh, would not be so distinctively vivid as when beheld

through the transfixing medium of George Eliot's
genius.   For here we have the personages, with all
their quaintnesses, their eccentricities, their odd, old-
fashioned twists and ways—only observed by fragments in actual life—successfully brought to a focus for
the delight and amusement of generations of readers.
There is nothing grotesque, nothing exaggerated, in
these humorous figures.   The comic effect is not
produced, as is often the case with the inventions of
Dickens, by some set peculiarity of manner or trick
of speech, more in the spirit of caricature.   On the
contrary, it is by a strict adherence to the just mean
of nature, by a conscientious care not to overstep her
probabilities, that we owe these matchless types of
English provincial life.   And the genuine humour
of these types verges on the pathetic, in that the
infinitely little of their lives is so magnified by them
out of all proportion to its real importance.   Mrs.
Glegg, with her dictatorial ways, her small economies,
her anxiety to make a handsome figure in her will,
and her invariable reference to what was " the way in
our family," as a criterion of right behaviour on
all occasions : Mrs. Pullet, the wife of the well-to-do
yeoman-farmer, bent on proving her gentility and
wealth by the delicacy of her health, and the quantity
of doctor's stuff she can afford to imbibe : Mrs.
Tulliver, the good, muddle-headed woman, whose
husband "picked her from her sisters o' purpose,
'cause she was a bit weak, like," and for whom the
climax of misery in bankruptcy is the loss of her
china and table-linen : these, as well as the hen-
pecked Mr. Glegg, and the old-maidish Mr. Pullet,
are worthy pendants to Mrs. Poyser and Dolly
Winthrop.

Whether too great a predominance may not be given to the narrow, trivial views of these people, with their prosaic respectability, is a nice question, which one is inclined to answer in the negative on reading such a conjugal scene as that between Mr. and Mrs. Glegg, after the latter's quarrel with Mr. Tulliver:

"It was a hard case that a vigorous mood for quarrelling, so highly capable of using any opportunity, should not meet with a single remark from Mr. Glegg on which to exercise itself. But by-and-by it appeared that his silence would answer the purpose, for he heard himself apostrophised at last in that tone peculiar to the wife of one's bosom.

"'Well, Mr. Glegg! it's a poor return I get for making you the wife I've made you all these years. If this is the way I'm to be treated, I'd better ha' known it before my poor father died, and then when I'd wanted a home, I should ha' gone elsewhere—as the choice was offered me.'

"Mr. Glegg paused from his porridge and looked up, not with any new amazement, but simply with that quiet, habitual wonder with which we regard constant mysteries.

"'Why, Mrs. G., what have I done now?'

"'Done now, Mr. Glegg? *done now?* . . . I'm sorry for you.'

"Not seeing his way to any pertinent answer, Mr. Glegg reverted to his porridge.

"'There's husbands in the world,' continued Mrs. Glegg, after a pause, 'as 'ud have known how to do something different to siding with everybody else against their own wives. Perhaps I'm wrong, and you can teach me better. But I've allays heard as it's the husband's place to stand by the wife, instead of rejoicing and triumphing when folks insult her."

"'Now what call have you to say that?' said Mr. Glegg rather warmly, for, though a kind man, he was not as meek as Moses. 'When did I rejoice or triumph over you?'

"'There's ways o' doing things worse than speaking out plain, Mr. Glegg. I'd sooner you'd tell me to my face as you make light of me, than try to make as everybody's in the right but me, and come to your breakfast in the morning, as I've hardly slept an hour this night, and sulk at me as if I was e dirt under your feet.'

"'Sulk at you?' said Mr. Glegg, in a tone of angry facetiousness. 'You're like a tipsy man as thinks everybody's had too much but himself.'

"'Don't lower yourself with using coarse language to *me*, Mr. Glegg! It makes you look very small, though you can't see yourself,' said Mrs. Glegg, in a tone of energetic compassion. 'A man in your place should set an example, and talk more sensible.'"

After a good deal of sparring in the same tone, Mr. Glegg at last bursts forth: "'Did ever anybody hear the like i' this parish? A woman with everything provided for her, and allowed to keep her own money the same as if it was settled on her, and with a gig new stuffed and lined at no end o' expense, and provided for when I die beyond anything she could expect ....to go on i' this way, biting and snapping like a mad dog! It's beyond everything, as God A'mighty should ha' made women *so*.' (These last words were uttered in a tone of sorrowful agitation. Mr. Glegg pushed his tea from him, and tapped the table with both his hands.)

"'Well, Mr. Glegg! if those are your feelings, it's best they should be known,' said Mrs. Glegg, taking off her napkin, and folding it in an excited manner. 'But if you talk o' my being provided for beyond what I could expect, I beg leave to tell you as I'd a right to expect a many things as I don't find. And as to my being like a mad dog, it's well if you're not cried shame on by the country for your treatment of me, for it's what I can't bear, and I won't bear.' . . .

"Here Mrs. Glegg's voice intimated that she was going to cry, and, breaking off from speech, she rang the bell violently.

"'Sally,' she said, rising from her chair, and speaking in rather a choked voice, 'light a fire upstairs, and put the blinds down. Mr. Glegg, you'll please order what you like for dinner. I shall have gruel.'"

Equally well drawn in their way, though belonging to a different class of character, are Maggie's cousin, the lovely, gentle, and refined Lucy; Philip Wakem, whose physical malformation is compensated by exceptional culture and nobility of nature; Mr. Tulliver, the headstrong, violent, but withal generous, father of Maggie, and his sister Mrs. Moss, whose motherliness and carelessness of appearances form a striking foil to the Dodson sisters. Indeed, 'The Mill on the Floss' is so rich in minor characters that it is impossible to do more than mention such capital sketches as that of Bob Jakin and his dog Mumps, or of Luke, the head miller, who has no opinion of reading, considering that "There's fools enoo—an' rogues enoo—wi'out lookin' i' books for 'em."

The distinguishing feature of this novel, however,

lies not so much in its wealth of portraiture or freshness of humour as in a certain passionate glow of
youth, which emanates from the heroine, and seems
to warm the story through and through. For passion,
pathos, and poetic beauty of description, 'The Mill
on the Floss' is certainly unique among George Eliot's
works.

CHAPTER X.

SILAS MARNER.

THE 'Mill on the Floss,' which appeared in 1860, fully established George Eliot's popularity with the public. In the same year she published anonymously, in *Blackwood's Magazine*, a short story called the 'Lifted Veil.' This tale is curious as differing considerably from her general style, having a certain mystical turn, which perhaps recommended it more especially to the admiration of Bulwer Lytton ; but, indeed, it attracted general attention. In the meanwhile, the relations between author and publisher became more and more friendly ; the latter's critical acumen and sound judgment being highly esteemed by George Eliot. " He judged well of writing," she remarked, " because he had learned to judge well of men and things, not merely through quickness of observation and insight, but with the illumination of a heart in the right place."

This was the most productive period of George Eliot's life. In three successive years she published 'Adam Bede,' 'The Mill on the Floss,' and 'Silas Marner,' the last story appearing in 1861. When the amount of thought, observation, and wisdom concentrated in these novels is taken into consideration, it must be admitted that her mental energy was truly astonishing. But it was the accumulated experience of her whole past, the first abundant math borne by the springtide of life which was garnered up in these three remarkable works. Afterwards, when she came to write her next book, 'Romola,' she turned to entirely fresh fields of inspiration ; indeed, already at this date her mind was occupied with the idea of an Italian novel of the time of Savonarola.

In the meanwhile she produced her most perfect work. She wrote 'Silas Marner, the Weaver of Rave-loe.' I call 'Silas Marner' her most perfect work, not only because of the symmetry with which each part is adjusted in relation to. the whole, nor be-cause of the absence of those partly satirical, partly moral reflections with which George Eliot usually accompanies the action of her stories, but chiefly on account of the simple pathos of the central motive into which all the different incidents and characters naturally converge. How homely are the elements from which this work of art is constructed, and how matchless the result !

Nothing but the story of a humble weaver be-longing to a small dissenting community which assembled in Lantern Yard, somewhere in the back streets of a manufacturing town ; of a faithless love and a false friend, and the loss of trust in all things human or divine. Nothing but the story of a lone, bewildered man, shut out from his kind, concentrating every baulked passion into one—the all-engrossing passion for gold. And then the sudden disappear-ance of the hoard from its accustomed hiding-place, and in its stead the startling apparition of a golden-haired little child, found one snowy winter's night sleeping on the floor in front of the glimmering hearth. And the gradual reawakening of love in the heart of the solitary man, a love ".drawing his hope and joy continually onward beyond the money," and once more bringing him into sympathetic relations with his fellow-men.

"In old days," says the story, "there were angels who came and took men by the hand and led them away from the city of destruction. We see no white-winged angels now. But yet men are led away from threatening destruction ;. a hand is put into theirs, which leads them :forth gently towards a calm and bright land, so that they look no more backward; and the hand may be a little child's.".

Curiously enough, I came quite recently upon a story. which in its leading features very closely resembles this tale of the 'Weaver of Raveloe.' It is called 'Jermola the Potter,' and is considered the masterpiece of J. I. Kraszewski, the Polish novelist, author of at least one hundred and fifty works in different branches of literature. 'Jermola,' the most popular of them all, has been translated into French, Dutch, and German. It gives an extraordinarily vivid picture of peasant life in a remote Polish village, and not only of peasant life, but of the manners and habits of the landed proprietor, the Jew, the artisan, and the yeoman, in a community whose modes of life have undergone but little modification since the Middle Ages. These pictures, though not elaborated with anything like the minute care of George Eliot's descriptions of English country life, yet from their extreme simplicity produce a most powerful impression on the reader.

The story, in brief, is that of Jermola, the body servant of a Polish nobleman in Volhynia, whom he

has served with rare devotion during the greater part
of his life.   Left almost a beggar at his master's
death, without a single human tie, all he can get for
years of faithful service is a tumble-down, forsaken
old inn, where he manages to keep body and soul
together in a dismantled room that but partly shelters
him from the inclemency of the weather.   Hopeless,
aimless, loveless, he grows old before his time, and
the passing of the days affects him hardly more than
it does a stone.   But one evening, as he is sitting in
front of a scanty fire repeating the Lord's Prayer, the
cry as of a little child startles him from his devotion.
Going to look what can be the meaning of such
unusual sounds, he soon discovers an infant in linen
swaddling-clothes wailing under an old oak tree.   He
takes the foundling home, and from that moment a
new life enters the old man's breast.   He is rejuvenated
by twenty years.   He is kept in a constant flutter
of hope, fear, and activity.   A kind-hearted woman,
called the Kozaczicha, tenders him her services, but
he is so jealous of any one but himself doing aught
for the child, that he checks her advances, and by
hook or by crook obtains a goat from an extortionate
Jew, by the help of which he rears the boy satisfactorily.   Then, wishing to make a livelihood for the
child's sake, he inclines at first to the craft of the
weaver, but finally turns potter in his old age.   Love
sharpening his wits, he plies quite a thriving trade in
time, and the beautiful boy brings him into more
friendly relations with his neighbours.   But one day,
when Radionek, who has learned Jermola's trade, is
about twelve years old, the real parents appear and
claim him as their own.   They had never dared to
acknowledge their marriage till the father, who had

threatened to disinherit his son in such an event, had departed this life. Now, having nothing more to fear, they want to have their child back, and to bring him up as befits their station in life. Jermola suffers a deadly anguish at this separation ; the boy, too, is in despair, for he clings fondly to the old man who has reared him with more than a father's love. But the parents insisting on their legal rights, Radionek is at last carried off to their house in town, to be turned into a gentleman, being only grudgingly allowed to see Jermola from time to time. The boy pines, however, for the dear familiar presence of his foster-father, and the free outdoor life, and at last, after some years of misery, he appears one day suddenly in Jermola's hut, who has given up his pottery in order to be secretly near the child he is afraid to go and see. The piteous entreaties of Radionek, and the sight of his now sickly countenance, induce the old man to flee into the pathless forests, where the two may escape unseen, and reach some distant part of the country to take up their old pleasant life once more. But the hardships and fatigues of the journey are too much for the boy's enfeebled health, and just as they come within sight of human dwellings, he is seized with a fever which cuts his young life short, leaving Jermola nearly crazy with anguish. Long afterwards a little decrepit old man was to be seen by churchgoers sitting near a grave, whom the children mocked by calling the "bony little man," because he seemed to consist of nothing but bones.

Such is the bare outline of a story whose main idea, that of the redemption of a human soul from cold, petrifying isolation, by means of a little child, is unquestionably the same as in 'Silas Marner.' Other incidents, such as that of the peasant woman who initiates Jermola into the mysteries of baby management, and the disclosure of the real parents after a lapse of years, wanting to have their child back, suggest parallel passages in the English book. But coincidences of this kind are, after all, natural enough, considering that the circle of human feeling and action is limited, and that in all ages and countries like conditions must give rise to much the same sequence of events. It is therefore most likely that George Eliot never saw, and possibly never even heard of, 'Jermola the Potter.'

The monotonous tone in the narrative of this Polish novel is in strong contrast, it may be observed, to George Eliot's vivid and varied treatment of her subject. This monotony, however, suits the local colouring of 'Jermola,' by suggesting the idea of the league-long expanse of ancient forests whose sombre solitudes encompass with a mysterious awe the little temporary dwellings of men. But if the foreign story surpasses 'Silas Marner' in tragic pathos, the latter far excels it in the masterly handling of character and dialogue, in the underlying breadth of thought, and, above all, in the precious salt of its humour. Indeed, for humour, for sheer force, for intense realism, George Eliot, in the immortal scene at the "Rainbow," may be said to rival Shakespeare. Her farriers, her butchers, her wheelwrights, her tailors, have the same startling vitality, the same unmistakable accents of nature, the same distinctive yet unforced individuality, free from either exaggeration or carica-ture. How delicious is the description of the party assembled in the kitchen of that inn, whose landlord—a strong advocate for compromising whatever differ-

ences of opinion may arise between his customers, as
beings "all alike in need of liquor"—clinches all arguments by his favourite phrase—"You're both right and
you're both wrong, as I say." How admirably comic
are these villagers, invariably beginning their nightly
sittings by a solemn silence, in which one and all puff
away at their pipes, staring at the fire "as if a bet
were depending on the first man who winked." And
when they begin at last, how rich is the flavour of
that talk, given with an unerring precision that forth-
with makes one acquainted with the crass ignorance
and shrewdness, the mother-wit and superstition, so
oddly jumbled together in the villager's mind. What
sublime absence of all knowledge of his native land is
shown by the veteran parish clerk, Mr. Macey, in
speaking of a person from another county which
apparently could not be so very different "from this
country, for he brought a fine breed o' sheep with
him, so there must be pastures there, and everything
reasonable." Yet the same man can put down youthful presumption pretty sharply, as when he remarks:
"There's allays two 'pinions; there's the 'pinion a
man has o' himsen, and there's the 'pinion other folks
have on him. There'd be two 'pinions about a cracked
bell, if the bell could hear itself."

Dolly Winthrop, the wife of the jolly wheelwright
who makes one of the company at the "Rainbow," is
no less admirable. She is not cut after any particular
pattern or type of human nature, but has a distinctive individuality, and is full of a freshness and un-
expectedness which sets foregone conclusions at de-
fiance. A notable woman, with a boundless appetite
for work, so that, rising at half-past four, she has "a
bit o' time to spare most days, for when one gets up

betimes i' the morning the clock seems to stan' still
tow'rt ten, afore it's time to go about the victual."
Yet with all this energy she is not shrewish, but a
calm, grave woman, in much request in sick rooms or
wherever there is trouble. . She is good-looking, too,
and of a comfortable temper, being patiently tolerant
of her husband's jokes, "considering that 'men would
be so,' and viewing the stronger sex 'in the light of
animals whom it pleased Heaven to make troublesome
like bulls or turkey cocks.' "

Her vague idea, shared indeed by Silas, that he
has quite another faith from herself, as coming from
another part of .the country, gives a vivid idea of
remote rural life, as well as her own dim, semi-pagan
but thoroughly reverential religious feelings, prompting her always to speak of the Divinity in the plural,
as when she says to Marner : "I've looked for help
in the right quarter, and give myself up to Them as
we must all give ourselves up to at the last ; and if
we'n done our part, it isn't to be believed as Them as
are above us 'ull be worse nor we are, and come short
o' Theirn."

The humour shown in these scenes and characters,
or, more properly speaking, George Eliot's humour in
general, belongs to the highest order, the same as
Shakespeare's. It is based on the essential elements
of human nature itself, on the pathetic incongruities
of which that "quintessence of dust," man, is made
up, instead of finding the comic in the purely accidental or external circumstances of life, as is the case
with such humourists as Rabelais and Dickens.
These latter might find a good subject for their
comic vein in seeing the Venus of Milo's broken
nose, which a mischievous urchin had again stuck on

the wrong side upwards—a sight to send the ordinary
spectator into fits of laughter. But the genuine
humourist sees something in that feature itself, as
nature shaped it, to excite his facetiousness. In 'A
Minor Prophet' some lines occur in which a somewhat similar view of the genuine source of humour is
pithily put :

"My yearnings fail
To reach that high apocalyptic mount
Which shows in bird's-eye view a perfect world,
Or enter warmly into other joys
Than those of faulty, struggling human kind.
That strain upon my soul's too feeble wing
Ends in ignoble floundering : I fall
Into short-sighted pity for the men
Who, living in those perfect future times,
Will not know half the dear imperfect things
That move my smiles and tears—will never know
The fine old incongruities that raise
My friendly laugh ; the innocent conceits
That like a needless eyeglass or black patch
Give those who wear them harmless happiness ;
The twists and cracks in our poor earthenware,
That touch me to more conscious fellowship
(I am not myself the finest Parian)
With my coevals."

Again, in her essay on 'Heinrich Heine,' George
Eliot thus defines the difference between humour and
wit : "Humour is of earlier growth than wit, and it is
in accordance with this earlier growth that it has more
affinity with the poetic tendencies, while wit is more
nearly allied to the ratiocinative intellect. Humour
draws its materials from situations and characteristics ;
wit seizes on unexpected and complex relations. . . .
It is only the ingenuity, condensation, and instan-
taneousness which lift some witticisms from reasoning

L

into wit ; they are reasoning raised to its highest power. On the other hand, humour, in its higher forms and in proportion as it associates itself with the sympathetic emotions, continually passes into poetry : nearly all great modern humorists may be called prose poets."

The quality which distinguishes George Eliot's humour may be said to characterise her treatment of human nature generally. In her delineations of life she carefully eschews the anomalous or exceptional, pointing out repeatedly that she would not, if she could, be the writer, however brilliant, who dwells by preference on the moral or intellectual attributes which mark off his hero from the crowd instead of on those which he has in common with average humanity. Nowhere perhaps in her works do we find this tendency so strikingly illustrated as in the one now under consideration ; for here we have the study of a human being who, by stress of circumstances, developes into a most abnormal specimen of mankind, yet who is brought back to normal conditions and to wholesome relations with his fellow-men by such a natural process as the re-awakening of benumbed sympathies through his love for the little foundling child. The scene where he finds that child has only been touched on in a passing allusion, yet there is no more powerfully-drawn situation in any of her novels than that where Silas, with the child in his arms, goes out into the dark night, and, guided by the little footprints in the virgin snow, discovers the dead mother, Godfrey Cass's opium-eating wife, lying with "her head sunk low in the furze and half covered with the shaken snow." There is a picture of this subject by the young and singularly gifted artist, the late Oliver Madox Brown, more generally known as a novelist, which is one of the few pictorial interpretations that seem to completely project on the canvas a visible embodiment of the spirit of the original. The pale, emaciated weaver, staring with big, short-sighted eyes at the body of the unconscious young woman stretched on the ground, clutching the lusty, struggling child with one arm, while with the other he holds a lantern which throws a feeble gleam on the snow—is realised with exceptional intensity.

The exquisite picture of Eppie's childhood, the dance she leads her soft-hearted foster-father are things to read, not to describe, unless one could quote whole pages of this delightful idyl, which for gracious charm and limpid purity of description re-calls those pearls among prose-poems, George Sand's 'François le Champi' and 'La Mare au Diable.'

CHAPTER XI.

ROMOLA.

'ROMOLA' marks a new departure in George Eliot's
literary career. From the present she turned to the
past, from the native to the foreign, from the domestic
to the historical. Yet in thus shifting her subject-
matter, she did not alter the strongly-pronounced
tendencies underlying her earlier novels; there was
more of spontaneous, humorous description of life in
the latter, whereas in 'Romola' the ethical teaching
which forms so prominent a feature of George
Eliot's art, though the same in essence, was more distinctly wrought out. Touching on this very point, she
observes in a letter to an American correspondent:
" It is perhaps less irrelevant to say, apropos of a distinction you seem to make between my earlier and
later works, that though I trust there is some growth
in my appreciation of others and in my self-distrust,
there has been no change in the point of view from
which I regard our life since I wrote my first fiction,
the 'Scenes of Clerical Life.' Any apparent change
of spirit must be due to something of which I am
unconscious. The principles which are at the root of
my effort to paint Dinah Morris are equally at the
root of my effort to paint Mordecai."
   The first section of 'Romola' appeared in the

Cornhill Magazine for the summer of 1862, and, running its course in that popular periodical, was finished in the summer of the following year. Mr. Lewes, in a letter writen from 16 Blandford Square, July 5, 1862, to some old friends of George Eliot, makes the following remarks in reference to this new form of publication : " My main object in persuading her to consent to serial publication, was not the unheard-of magnificence of the offer, but the advantage to such a work of being read slowly and deliberately, instead of being galloped through in three volumes. I think it quite unique, and so will the public when it gets over the first feeling of surprise and disappointment at the book not being English, and like its predecessor." And some time afterwards he wrote to the same friends : " Marian lives entirely in the fifteenth century, and is much cheered every now and then by hearing indirectly how her book is appreciated by the higher class of minds, and some of the highest ; though it is not, and cannot be popular. In Florence we hear they are wild with delight 'and surprise at such a work being executed by a foreigner ; as if an Italian had ever done anything of the kind !"

Before writing 'Romola' George Eliot had spent six weeks in Florence in order to familiarise herself with the manners and conversation of its inhabitants, and yet she hardly caught the trick of Italian speech, and for some time afterwards she hung back from beginning her story, as her characters not only refused to speak Italian to her, but would not speak at all, as we can well imagine Mrs. Poyser, Bartle Massey, and Maggie to have done. These recalcitrant spirits were at last brought to order, and she succeeded so well, especially in her delineation of the lower classes, that they have been recognised by Italians as true to the life.

It should, however, be mentioned that the greatest modern Italian, Giuseppe Mazzini, found fault with the handling, and, indeed, with the introduction into this novel of the great figure of Savonarola. He considered that it compared unfavourably with 'Adam Bede,' a novel he genuinely admired, all but the marriage of Adam with Dinah Morris, which, he said, shocked his feelings, not having any conception that the taste of the novel-reading public demands a happy ending whatever may have been the previous course of the three volumes. Another illustrious man, D. G. Rossetti, whose judgment on such a subject carries peculiar weight, considered George Eliot to have been much less successful in 'Romola' than in her novels of English country life. He did not think that the tone and colour of Italian life in the fifteenth century were caught with that intuitive perception of a bygone age characteristic of a Walter Scott or a Meinhold. The Florentine contemporaries of "Fra Girolamo" seemed to him Nineteenth Century men and women dressed up in the costume of the Fifteenth. The book, to use his expression, was not "native."

It is a majestic book, however: the most grandly planned of George Eliot's novels. It has a certain architectural dignity of structure, quite in keeping with its Italian nationality, a quality, by the way, entirely absent from the three later novels. The impressive historical background is not unlike one of Mr. Irving's magnificently wrought Italian stage-effects, rich in movement and colour, yet helping to throw the chief figures into greater relief. The

erudition shown in this work; the vast yet minute
acquaintance with the habits of thought, the manners,
the very talk of the Florentines of that day are truly
surprising; but perhaps the very fact of that erudition
being so perceptible shows that the material has
not been absolutely vitalised. The amount of labour
George Eliot expended on 'Romola' was so great,
that it was the book which, she remarked to a friend,
"she began a young woman and ended an old one."
The deep impression her works had made upon the
public mind heightened her natural conscientiousness,
and her gratitude for the confidence with which each
fresh contribution from her pen was received, increased
her anxiety to wield her influence for the highest
ends.

But her gratitude to the public by no means
extended to the critics. She recoiled from them with
the instinctive shrinking of the sensitive plant. These
interpreters between author and public were in her
eyes a most superfluous modern institution : though
at one time she herself had not scorned to sit in the
critic's seat. It is well-known that G. H. Lewes
acted as a kind of moral screen protecting her from
every gust or breath of criticism that was not entirely
genial. One lady, after reading 'The Mill on the
Floss,' had written off in the heat of the moment,
and, with the freedom of old friendship, while expressing the warmest admiration for the beauty of
the first two volumes, she had ventured to find fault
with part of the third. This letter was returned by
Lewes, who begged her at the same time never to write
again in this strain to George Eliot, to whom he had
not ventured to show it for fear it should too painfully
affect her. In a letter to the American lady already

mentioned, George Eliot, after referring to this habit of Mr. Lewes, says : " In this way I get confirmed in my impression that the criticism of any new writing is shifting and untrustworthy.   I hardly think that any critic can have so keen a sense of the shortcomings in my works as that I groan under in ·the course of writing them, and I cannot imagine any edification coming to an author from a sort of reviewing which consists in attributing to him or her unexpressed opinions, and in imagining circumstances which may be alleged as petty private motives for the treatment of subjects which ought to be of general ; human interest.· .· . · I have been led into this rather super-fluous sort of remark by the mention of a rule which seemed to require explanation."

And again on another occasion to the same effect : " But do not expect criticism from me.   I hate 'sitting in the seat of judgment,' and I would rather impress the public generally with the sense that they may get the best result from a book without necessarily forming an ' opinion ' about it, than I would rush into stating opinions of my own.   The floods of nonsense printed in the form of critical opinions seem to me a chief curse of our times—a chief obstacle to true culture."

In spite of these severe strictures on the critics and their opinions, an " opinion " must now be given about ' Romola.'   This novel may really be judged from two entirely different points of view, possibly from others besides, but, as it appears to me, from two.   One may consider it as an historical work, with its moving pageants, its civic broils, its church festivals, its religious revival, its fickle populace, now siding with the Pope, and now with the would-be reformer of the Papacy. Or again one may regard the conjugal relations between Romola and Tito, the slow spiritual growth of the one, and the swifter moral disintegration of the other, as one of the subtlest studies in psychology in literature.

To turn to the scenic details which form a considerable element of this historical picture, I have already hinted that they are not without a taint of cumbrousness and pedantry. The author seems to move somewhat heavily under her weight of learning, and we miss that splendid natural swiftness and ease of movement which Shakespere, Goethe, and Hugo know how to impart to their crowds and spectacular effects. If, instead of the people, one examines the man who dominated the people, the large, massive, imposing figure of Savonarola, one must admit that the character is very powerfully and faithfully executed but not produced at one throw. He does not take the imagination by storm as he would have done had Carlyle been at his fashioning. With an epithet or two, with a sharp, incisive phrase, the latter would have conjured the great Dominican from his grave, and we should have seen him, or believed at least that we saw him, as he was in the flesh when his impassioned voice resounded through the Duomo, swaying the hearts of the Florentine people with the force of a great conviction. That he stands out thus tangibly in 'Romola' it would be futile to assert : nevertheless, he is a noble, powerful study, although one has laboriously to gather into one's mind the somewhat mechanical descriptions which help to portray his individuality. The idea underlying the working out of this grand character is the same which Goethe had once proposed to himself in his projected,

but unfortunately never executed, drama of 'Ma-
homet.' It is that of a man of moral genius, who, in
solitude and obscurity, has conceived some new, pro-
founder aspect of religious truth, and who, stirred by
a sublime devotion, now goes forth among men to
bless and regenerate them by teaching them this
higher life. But in his contact with the multitude, in
his efforts at influencing it, the prophet or preacher is
in his turn influenced. If he fails to move by the
loftiest means, he will gradually resort to the lower in
order to effect his purpose. The purity of his spirit
is tarnished, ambition has crept in where holiness
reigned, and his perfect rectitude of purpose will be
sacrificed so that he may but rule.

Such are the opposing tendencies co-existing in
Savonarola's mixed but lofty nature. For "that
dissidence between inward reality and outward seeming was not the Christian simplicity after which he
had striven through years of his youth and prime, and
which he had preached as a chief fruit of the Divine
life. In the heat and stress of the day, with cheeks
burning, with shouts ringing in the ears, who is so
blest as to remember the yearnings he had in the cool
and silent morning, and know that he has not belied
them?" And again: "It was the habit of Savonarola's mind to conceive great things, and to feel that
he was the man to do them. Iniquity should be
brought low; the cause of justice, purity, and love
should triumph, and it should triumph by his voice,
by his work, by his blood. In moments of ecstatic
contemplation, doubtless, the sense of self melted in
the sense of the Unspeakable, and in that part of his
experience lay the elements of genuine self-abasement;
but in the presence of his fellow-men for whom he

was to act, pre-eminence seemed a necessary condition of life." But, as George Eliot says, "Power rose against him, not because of his sins, but because of his greatness ; not because he sought to deceive the world, but because he sought to make it noble. And through that greatness of his he endured a double agony ; not only the reviling, and the torture, and the death-throe, but the agony of sinking from the vision of glorious achievement into that deep-shadow where he could only say, 'I count as nothing : darkness encompasses me ; yet the light I saw was the true light.'"

But after all, in George Eliot's story the chief interest attaching to "Fra Girolamo" consists in his influence on Romola's spiritual growth. This may possibly be a blemish ; yet in most novels the fictitious characters eclipse the historical ones. The effect produced by the high-souled Romola is not unlike that of an antique statue, at once splendidly beautiful and imposingly cold. By the side of Tito she reminds one of the pure whiteness of marble sculpture as contrasted with the rich glowing sensuousness of a Venetian picture.

It is difficult to analyse why the proud, loving, single-hearted Romola, who has something of the fierceness and impetuosity of the old "Bardo blood" in her, should leave this impression of coldness ; for in spite of her acts of magnanimity and self-devotion, such, curiously enough, is the case. Perhaps in this instance George Eliot modelled the character too much according to a philosophical conception instead of projecting it, complete in its incompleteness, as it might have come from the hand of Nature. Another objection sometimes brought forward, of Romola having but little resemblance to an Italian woman of the fifteenth century, seems to me less relevant. The lofty dignity, the pride, the intense adhesion to family traditions were, on the contrary, very marked attributes of a high national type during the period of Italian supremacy. In fact, the character is not without hints and suggestions of such a woman as Vittoria Colonna, while its didactic tendency slightly recalls "those awful women of Italy who held professorial chairs, and were great in civil and canon law." In one sense Romola is a true child of the Renaissance. Brought up by her father, the enthusiastic old scholar, in pagan ideas, she had remained aloof from Roman Catholic beliefs and superstitions, and even when transformed by the mighty influence of Savonarola into a devoted *Piagnone*, her attitude always remains more or less that of a Protestant, unwilling to surrender the right of private judgment to the Church.

The clash of character when a woman like Romola finds herself chained in a life-long bond to such a nature as Tito's—the beautiful, wily, insinuating Greek — is wrought out with wonderful skill and matchless subtlety of analysis. Indeed Tito is not only one of George Eliot's most original creations, he is a unique character in fiction. Novelists, as a rule, only depict the full-blown villain or traitor, their virtuous and wicked people being separated from each other by a hard and fast line much like the goats and sheep. They continually treat character as something permanent and unchangeable, whereas to George Eliot it presents itself as an organism flexible by nature, subject to change under varying conditions, liable on the one hand to disease and

deterioration, but on the other hand no less capable
of being rehabilitated, refined, or ennobled. This is
one of the most distinctive notes of George Eliot's
art, and gives a quickening, fructifying quality to her
moral teaching. But it is an artistic no less than
a moral gain, sharpening the interest felt in the
evolution of her fictitious personages. For this reason
Tito, the creature of circumstances, is perhaps the
most striking of all her characters in the eyes of the
psychologist. We seem to see the very pulse of
the human machine laid bare, to see the corroding
effect of self-indulgence and dread of pain on a nature
not intrinsically wicked, to see at last how, little by
little, weakness has led to falsehood, and falsehood to
infamy. And yet this creature, who, under our eyes,
gradually hardens into crime, is one so richly dowered
with rare gifts of person and mind, that in spite of his
moral degeneracy, he fascinates the reader no less
than the men and women supposed to come into
actual contact with him. His beauty is described
with the same life-like intensity as Hetty's : the
warm glow of colour in his perfectly-moulded face,
with its dark curls and long agate-like eyes; his
sunny brightness of look, the velvet softness of
a manner with which he ingratiates himself with
young and old, and the airy buoyancy of his whole
gracious being, are as vividly portrayed as the quick
talent to which everything comes natural, the abundant good-humour, the acuteness of a polished intellect, whose sharp edge, will, at need, cut relentlessly
through every tissue of sentiment.

From Melema's first uneasy debate with himself,
when, in his splendid, unsoiled youth, he enters
Florence a shipwrecked stranger—a debate, that is,

as to whether he is bound to go in search of Bal-
dassare, who has been as a father to him—to the
moment when his already blunted conscience absolves
him from such a search, and again, on to that supreme
crisis when, suddenly face to face with his benefactor,
he denies him, and so is inevitably urged from one
act of baseness and cruelty to another still blacker
—we have unfolded before us, by an unshrinking
analyzer of human nature, what might not inappro-
priately be called " A Soul's Tragedy."   The wonderful art in the working out of this character is shown
in the fact that one has no positive impression of
Tito's innate badness, but, on the contrary, feels as if,
after his first lapses from truth and goodness, there
is still a possibility of his reforming, if only his soft,
pleasure-loving nature were not driven on, almost in
spite of himself, by his shuddering dread of shame or
suffering in any form.   "For," writes George Eliot,
"Tito was experiencing that inexorable law of human
souls, that we prepare ourselves for sudden deeds by
the reiterated choice of good or evil which gradually
determines character."

The description of the married life of Romola and
Tito is unsurpassed in George Eliot's novels for
subtlety and depth of insight : notably the young
wife's fond striving after complete inner harmony, her
first, faint, unavowed sense of something wanting, her
instinctive efforts to keep fast hold of her love and
trust, and her violent, irrevocable recoil on the discovery of Tito's first faithless action.   Perhaps there
is something cold, almost stern, in Romola's loathing
alienation from her husband, and the instantaneous
death of her passionate love.   One cannot quite
hin   the impression that a softer woman might have

forgiven and won from him a confession of his wrong-
doing ; a confession which would have averted the
committal of his worst and basest deeds.   Indeed, it
is Tito's awe of his grand, noble wife, and his dread
of her judgment, which first of all incite him to pre-
varication and lies.

It is curious to compare George Sand's theory of
love, in this instance, with George Eliot's.   In ' Leon
Leoni,' and in many of her novels besides, the
Frenchwoman seems to imply that for a woman to
love once is to love always, and that there is nothing
so base, or mean, or cruel, but she will forgive the
man on whom she has placed her affections.   In the
story mentioned above she has worked out this idea
to an extent which, in many of its details, is simply
revolting.   Love is there described as a magnetic
attraction, unresisted and irresistible, to which the
heroine absolutely surrenders pride, reason, and conscience.   Just the opposite kind of love is that
which we find portrayed in ' Romola:' it is a love
identical with the fullest belief in the truth and
goodness of the beloved object, so that at the first
realisation of moral obliquity the repulsion created
extinguishes that love, although there is no outward
severance of the marriage bond.

This great novel closes with these significant words,
which Romola addresses to Lillo, Tito's child, but
not her own :

"And so, my Lillo, if you mean to act nobly, and
seek to know the best things God has put within
reach of man, you must learn to fix your mind on
that end, and not on what will happen to you because
of it.   And remember, if you were to choose something lower, and make it the rule of your life to seek

your own pleasure and escape from what is disagree-
able, calamity might come just the same ; and it
would be calamity falling on a base mind, which is
the one form of sorrow that has no balm in it, and
that may well make a man say, 'It would have been
better for me if I had never been born!'"

CHAPTER XII.

HER POEMS.

FEW are the external events to be now recorded
of George Eliot's life. The publication of her successive works forms the chief landmarks. But the
year 1865 is distinguished by circumstances of some
importance. In this year Mr. Lewes, after assisting
to found the *Fortnightly Review*, assumed its editorship ; and among the contributions to the first number
of the new Review was a short article from the pen
of George Eliot on Mr. Lecky's important work 'The
Influence of Rationalism.'

In the course of the same year Mr. and Mrs. Lewes
moved from 16 Blandford Square to the Priory, a
commodious house in North Bank, St. John's Wood,
which has come to be intimately associated with the
memory of George Eliot. Here, in the pleasant
dwelling-rooms decorated by Owen Jones, might be
met, at her Sunday afternoon receptions, some of the
most eminent men in literature, art, and science. For
the rest, her life flowed on its even tenor, its routine
being rigidly regulated. The morning till lunch time
was invariably devoted to writing : in the afternoon
she either went out for a quiet drive of about two
hours, or she took a walk with Lewes in Regent's
Park. There the strange-looking couple—she with

a certain weird, sibylline air, he not unlike some
unkempt Polish refugee of vivacious manners—might
be seen, swinging their arms, as they hurried along
at a pace as rapid and eager as their talk. Besides
these walks, George Eliot's chief recreation consisted
in frequenting concerts and picture galleries. To
music she was passionately devoted, hardly ever
failing to attend at the Saturday afternoon concerts
at St. James's Hall, besides frequenting various
musical réunions, such as the following extract from
one of her letters will show: "The other night we
went to hear the Bach choir—a society of ladies and
gentlemen got together by Jenny Lind, who sings in
the middle of them, her husband acting as conductor.
It is pretty to see people who might be nothing but
simply fashionables taking pains to sing fine music in
tune and time, with more or less success. One of
the baritones we know is a G——, who used to be
a swell guardsman, and has happily taken to good
courses while still quite young. Another is a handsome young G——, not of the unsatisfactory Co.,
but of the R—— G—— kin. A soprano is Mrs.
P——, wife of the Queen's Secretary, General P——,
the granddaughter of Earl Grey, and just like him in
the face—and so on. These people of 'high' birth
are certainly reforming themselves a little."

She likewise never omitted to visit the "Exhibition
of Old Masters" at Burlington House. To most
people few things exercise so great a strain on their
mental and physical powers of endurance as the
inspection of a picture gallery, with its incessant
appeal to the most concentrated attention. Yet, in
spite of physical weakness, George Eliot possessed
such inexhaustible mental energy that she could go

on, hour after hour, looking with the same unflagging
interest at whatever possessed any claim to attention,
tiring out even vigorous men that were in her company. In her works the allusions to art are much
less frequent than to music; but from a few hints
here and there, it is possible to form some idea of
her taste, one very significant passage in 'Adam
Bede' showing her peculiar love of Dutch paintings,
and her readiness to turn without shrinking "from
cloud-borne angels, from prophets, sibyls, and heroic
warriors, to an old woman bending over her flower-
pot, or eating her solitary dinner, while the noonday
light, softened perhaps by a screen of leaves, falls on
her mob-cap, and just touches the rim of her spinning-
wheel and her stone jug, and all those cheap common
things which are the precious necessaries of life
to her."

Another favourite resort of George Eliot's was the
Zoological Gardens. She went there a great deal to
study the animals, and was particularly fond of the
" poor dear ratel" that used to turn somersaults. In
fact her knowledge of, and sympathy with, animals
was as remarkable as that which she showed for
human nature. Thus she astonished a gentleman
farmer by drawing attention to the fine points of
his horses. Her intimate acquaintance with the dog
comes out in a thousand touches in her novels, and
her humorous appreciation of little pigs led her to
watch them attentively, and to pick out some particular favourite in every litter. In her country
rambles, too, she was fond of turning over stones to
inspect the minute insect life teeming in moist, dark
places; and she was as interested as Lewes himself
in the creatures, frogs, etc., he kept for scientific pur-

poses, and which would sometimes, like the frog in
the fairy tale, surprise the household by suddenly
making their entrance into the dining-room.   Her
liking for the "poor brutes," as she calls them, had
its origin no doubt in the same source of profound
pity which she feels for "the twists and cracks" of
imperfect human beings.

Her evenings were usually passed at home, and
spent in reading, or in playing and singing; but she
and Lewes used to go to the theatre on any occasion
of special interest, as when Salvini appeared in
' Othello,' a performance attended repeatedly by
both with enthusiastic delight.   Otherwise they
rarely left home, seldom visiting at other people's
houses, although they made an exception in the case
of a favoured few.

They were both fond of travelling, and, whenever
it was possible, would take trips to the Continent,
or seek some quiet English rural retreat away from
the sleepless tumult of London.   "For," says Lewes
incidentally in a letter, "Mrs. Lewes never seems
at home except under a broad sweep of sky and the
greenth of the uplands round her."   So we find them
frequently contriving a change of scene; and the
visits to foreign countries, the pleasant sauntering
on long summer days through Continental towns,
"dozing round old cathedrals," formed delightful
episodes in George Eliot's strenuously active life.
The residence in Germany in 1854, and again in
1858, has already been alluded to.   Now, in the
year 1865, they paid a short visit to France, in the
course of which they saw Normandy, Brittany, and
Touraine, returning much refreshed at the beginning
of the autumn.   Two years afterwards they went to

Spain, a country that must have possessed a peculiar interest for both; for in 1846 Lewes had published a charming, if one-sided, little book on 'The Spanish Drama,' with especial reference to Lope de Vega and Calderon; and in 1864, only a year after the appearance of 'Romola,' George Eliot produced the first draught of 'The Spanish Gypsy.' On becoming personally acquainted with this land of "old romance," however, her impressions were so far modified and deepened that she re-wrote and amplified her poem, which was not published till 1868.

The subject of the gypsies was probably suggested to George Eliot by her own memorable adventure in childhood, which thus became the germ of a very impressive poem. Be that as it may, it is worth noticing that the conception of 'The Spanish Gypsy' should have followed so closely on the completion of the Italian novel, both being foreign subjects, belonging to much the same period of history. In both the novelist has departed from her habitual track, seeking for "pastures new" in a foreign soil. After inculcating on the artist the desirability of giving "the loving pains of a life to the faithful representation of commonplace things," she remarks in 'Adam Bede' that "there are few prophets in the world, few sublimely beautiful women, few heroes," and that we cannot afford to give all our love and reverence to such rarities. But having followed this rule, and given the most marvellously truthful delineations of her fellow-men as they are ordinarily to be met with, she now also felt prompted to draw the exceptional types of human character, the rare prophets, and the sublime heroes.

To a literary friend George Eliot one day

mentioned a plan of giving "the world an ideal portrait of an actual character in history, whom she did not name, but to whom she alluded as an object of possible reverence unmingled with disappointment." This idea was never carried out, but at any rate Dinah Morris, Savonarola, Zarca, and Mordecai are all exceptional beings—beings engrossed by an impersonal aim, having the spiritual or national regeneration of their fellow-men for its object. Dinah and Savonarola are more of the nature of prophets; Zarca and Mordecai of that of patriots. Among these the fair Methodist preacher, whose yearning piety is only a more sublimated love of her kind, is the most vividly realised; while Mordecai, the patriot of an ideal country, is but the abstraction of a man, entirely wanting in that indefinable solidity of presentation which gives a life of its own to the creations of art.

On the whole, Zarca, the gipsy chief, is perhaps the most vividly drawn of George Eliot's purely ideal characters—characters which never have the flesh-and-blood reality of her Mrs. Poysers, her Silas Marners, and her dear little Totties and Eppies. Yet there is an unmistakable grandeur and power of invention in the heroic figure of Zarca, although, in spite of this power, we miss the convincing stamp of reality in him, and not only in him, but more or less in all the characters of the 'Spanish Gypsy.' George Eliot's feeling for the extraordinary and romantic was very subordinate to that which she entertained for the more familiar aspects of our life. For, although she here chose one of the most romantic of periods and localities, the Spain of Ferdinand and Isabella, with the mingled horror and magnificence

of its national traditions, she does not really succeed
in resuscitating the spirit which animated those
devout, cruel, fanatical, but ultra-picturesque times.
The Castilian noble, the Jewish astrologer, Zarca,
and the Spanish Inquisitor, even the bright, gloriously-
conceived Fedalma herself, think and speak too
much like sublimated modern positivists. For example, would, could, or should any gipsy of the
fifteenth century have expressed himself in the following terms :

> " Oh, it is a faith
> Taught by no priest, but by this beating heart :
> Faith to each other : the fidelity
> Of fellow-wanderers in a desert place,
> Who share the same dire thirst, and therefore share
> The scanty water : the fidelity
> Of men whose pulses leap with kindred fire,
> Who in the flash of eyes, the clasp of hands,
> The speech that even in lying tells the truth
> Of heritage inevitable as birth,
> Nay, in the silent bodily presence feel
> The mystic stirring of a common life
> Which makes the many one : fidelity
> To the consecrating oath our sponsor Fate
> Made through our infant breath when we were born
> The fellow-heirs of that small island, Life,
> Where we must dig and sow and reap with brothers.
> Fear thou that oath, my daughter—nay, not fear,
> But love it ; for the sanctity of oaths
> Lies not in lightning that avenges them,
> But in the injury wrought by broken bonds
> And in the garnered good of human trust."

The poetic mode of treatment corresponds to the
exalted theme of the 'Spanish Gypsy,' a subject certainly more fitted for drama or romance rather than
for the novel, properly so called. Nothing could
apparently be better adapted for the purposes of a

noble, historical poem than the conception of a great
man such as Zarca, whose aim is nothing less than
the fusion of the scattered, wandering, lawless gypsy
tribes into one nation, with common traditions and a
common country : the romantic incident of the discovery of his lost daughter in the affianced bride of
Silva, Duke of Bedmar : the supreme conflict in
Fedalma's breast between love and duty, her renunciation of happiness in order to cast in her lot with
that of her outcast people : Silva's frantic grief, his
desertion of his country, his religion, and all his
solemn responsibilities to turn gypsy for Fedalma's
sake, and having done so, his agony of remorse on
seeing the fortress committed to his trust taken by
the gypsies he has joined, his dearest friends mas-
sacred, his nearest of kin, Isidor, the inquisitor,
hanged before his very eyes, a sight so maddening
that, hardly conscious of his act, he slays Zarca, and
so divides himself for ever, by an impassable gulf, from
the woman for whose sake he had turned apostate.

Clearly a subject containing the highest capabilities,
and, if great thoughts constituted a great poem, this
should be one of the greatest.   But with all its
high merits, its sentiments imbued with rare moral
grandeur, its felicitous descriptions, the work lacks
that best and incommunicable gift which comes by
nature to the poet.   Here, as in her novels, we find
George Eliot's instinctive insight into the primary
passions of the human heart, her wide sympathy and
piercing keenness of vision ; but her thoughts, instead of being naturally winged with melody, seem
mechanically welded into song.   This applies to all
her poetic work, although some of it, especially the
'Legend of Jubal,' reaches a much higher degree of

metrical and rhythmical excellence. But although George Eliot's poems cannot be considered on a par with her prose, they possess a distinctive interest, and should be carefully studied by all lovers of her genius, as affording a more intimate insight into the working of her own mind. Nowhere do we perceive so clearly as here the profound sadness of her view of life ; nowhere does she so emphatically reiterate the stern lesson of the duty of resignation and self-sacrifice ; or that other doctrine that the individual is bound absolutely to subordinate his personal happiness to the social good, that he has no rights save the right of fulfilling his obligations to his age, his country, and his family. This idea is perhaps more completely incorporated in Fedalma than in any other of her characters — Fedalma, who seems so bountifully endowed with the fullest measure of beauty, love and happiness, that her renunciation may be the more absolute. She who, in her young joy suddenly knows herself as "an aged sorrow," exclaiming :

" I will not take a heaven
Haunted by shrieks of far-off misery.
This deed and I have ripened with the hours :
It is a part of me—a wakened thought
That, rising like a giant, masters me,
And grows into a doom. O mother life,
That seemed to nourish me so tenderly,
Even in the womb you vowed me to the fire,
Hung on my soul the burden of men's hopes,
And pledged me to redeem !—I'll pay the debt.
You gave me strength that I should pour it all
Into this anguish. I can never shrink
Back into bliss—my heart has grown too big
With things that might be."

This sacrifice is the completer for being without

hope ; for not counting "on aught but being faithful;" for resting satisfied in such a sublime conviction as—

> "The grandest death, to die in vain—for love
> Greater than sways the forces of the world."

Limit forbids me dwell longer on this poem, which contains infinite matter for discussion, yet some of the single passages are so full of fine thoughts felicitously expressed that it would be unfair not to allude to them. Such a specimen as this exposition of the eternal dualism between the Hellenic and the Christian ideals, of which Heine was the original and incomparable expounder, should not be left unnoted:

> "For evermore
> With grander resurrection than was feigned
> Of Attila's fierce Huns, the soul of Greece
> Conquers the bulk of Persia. The maimed form
> Of calmly-joyous beauty, marble-limbed,
> Yet breathing with the thought that shaped its limbs,
> Looks mild reproach from out its opened grave
> At creeds of terror ; and the vine-wreathed god
> Fronts the pierced Image with the crown of thorns."

And again how full of deep mysterious suggestion is this line—

> "Speech is but broken light upon the depth
> Of the unspoken."

And this grand saying—

> "What times are little ? To the sentinel
> That hour is regal when he mounts on guard."

Quotations of this kind might be indefinitely multiplied ; while showing that exaltation of thought properly belonging to poetry, they at the same time indubitably prove to the delicately-attuned ear the absence of that subtle intuitive music, that "linked sweetness" of sound and sense which is the birthright of poets. If an intimate and profound acquaintance with the laws and structure of metre could bestow this quality, which appertain to the elemental, George Eliot's verse ought to have achieved the highest success. For in mere technical knowledge concerning rhyme, assonance, alliteration, and the manipulation of blank verse according to the most cunning distribution of pauses, she could hold her own with the foremost contemporary poets, being no doubt far more versed than either Shelley or Byron in the laws governing these matters.

How incalculable she felt the poet's influence to be, and how fain she would have had him wield this influence only for the loftiest ends, is well shown in a beautiful letter, hitherto unpublished, now possessing an added pathos as addressed to one who has but lately departed, at the very time when his rare poetic gifts were beginning to be more widely recognised. James Thomson, the author of "The City of Dreadful Night," a poem which appeared first in the pages of the 'National Reformer,' with the signature of "B. V.," was thus addressed by George Eliot :

"Dear Poet, — I cannot rest satisfied without telling you that my mind responds with admiration to the distinct vision and grand utterance in the poem which you have been so good as to send me.

" Also, I trust that an intellect informed by so much passionate energy as yours will soon give us more heroic strains, with a wider embrace of human fellowship, such as will be to the labourers of the world what the Odes of Tyrtæus were to the

Spartans, thrilling them with the sublimity of the social order and the courage of resistance to all that would dissolve it. To accept life and write much fine poetry, is to take a very large share in the quantum of human good, and seems to draw with it necessarily some recognition, affectionate, and even joyful, of the manifold willing labours which have made such a lot possible."

These words are of peculiar interest, because, although the writer of them is almost as much of a pessimist as its recipient, they are so with a difference. The pessimism of "The City of Dreadful Night," in its blank hopelessness, paralyses the inmost nerve of life by isolating the individual in cold obstruction. Whereas George Eliot, while recognising to the utmost "the burthen of a world, where even the sunshine has a heart of care," insists the more on the fact that this common suffering binds man more indissolubly to man ; that so far from justifying him in ending his life "when he will," the groaning and travailing generations exact that he should stand firm at his post, regardless of personal consideration or requital, so long only as he can help towards making the fate of his fellow mortals less heavy for them to bear. In fact, the one is a theory of life, the other a disease of the soul.

The same stoic view, in a different form, finds expression in this answer to a dear friend's query : "I cannot quite agree that it is hard to see what has been the good of your life. It seems to me very clear that you have been a good of a kind that would have been sorely missed by those who have been nearest to you, and also by some who are more distant. And it is this kind of good which must reconcile us to life, and not any answer to the question, 'What would the universe have been without me?' The point one has to care for is, 'Are A, B, and C the better for me?' And there are several letters of the alphabet that could not have easily spared you in the past, and that can still less spare you in the present."

This lesson of resignation, which is enforced more and more stringently in her writings, is again dwelt upon with peculiar emphasis in the interesting dramatic sketch entitled 'Armgart.' The problem here is not unlike that in 'Silas Marner.' It is that of an individual, in exceptional circumstances, brought back to the average condition of humanity; but whereas Silas, having sunk below the common standard, is once more united to his fellow-men by love, the magnificently endowed Armgart, who seems something apart and above the crowd, is reduced to the level of the undistinguished million by the loss of her peerless voice. 'Armgart' is the single instance, excepting, perhaps, the Princess Halm-Eberstein, where George Eliot has attempted to depict the woman-artist, to whom life's highest object consists in fame—

> " The benignant strength of one, transformed
> To joy of many."

But in the intoxicating flush of success, the singer, who has refused the love of *one* for that " sense transcendent which can taste the joy of swaying multitudes," loses her glorious gift, and so sinks irretrievably to a " drudge among the crowd." In the first delirium of despair she longs to put an end to herself, "sooner than bear the yoke of thwarted life;"

but is painfully startled from her defiant mood by the indignant query of Walpurga, her humble cousin—

> " Where is the rebel's right for you alone?
>   Noble rebellion lifts a common load ;
>   But what is he who flings his own load off
>   And leaves his fellows toiling ?   Rebel's right?
>   Say rather the deserter's.   Oh, you smiled
>   From your clear height on all the million lots
>   Which yet you brand as abject."

It may seem singular that having once, in 'Arm-gart,' drawn a woman of the highest artistic aims and ambitions, George Eliot should imply that what is most valuable in her is not the exceptional gift, but rather that part of her nature which she shares with ordinary humanity. This is, however, one of her leading beliefs, and strongly contrasts her, as a teacher, with Carlyle. To the author of ' Hero Worship ' the promiscuous mass—moiling and toiling as factory hands and artisans, as miners and labourers —only represents so much raw material, from which is produced that final result and last triumph of the combination of human forces—the great statesman, great warrior, great poet, and so forth. To George Eliot, on the contrary—and this is the democratic side of her nature—it is the multitude, so charily treated by destiny, which claims deepest sympathy and tenderest compassion ; so that all greatness, in her eyes, is not a privilege, but a debt, which entails on its possessor a more strenuous effort, a completer devotion to the service of average humanity.

CHAPTER XIII.

FELIX HOLT AND MIDDLEMARCH.

IN 'Felix Holt,' which was published in 1866, George Eliot returned once more to her own peculiar field, where she stands supreme and unrivalled—the novel of English provincial life. This work, which, however, is not equal to her earlier or later fictions, yet possesses a double interest for us. It is the only one of her writings from which its author's political views may be inferred, if we exclude a paper published in *Blackwood's Magazine* in January 1868, which, indeed, seems to be part of the novel, seeing that it is entitled, "Address to Working Men, by Felix Holt." The paper contains, in a more direct and concise form, precisely the same general views as regards the principles of government which were previously enunciated through Felix the Radical. It was an appeal to the operative classes who had been only recently enfranchised by the Reform Bill. Its advice is mainly to the effect that genuine political and social improvements to be durable must be the result of inward change rather than of outward legislation. The writer insists on the futility of the belief that beneficial political changes can be effected by revolutionary measures. She points out the necessity of a just discrimination between what is curable in the body politic and what has to be endured. She dwells once again, with solemn insistence, on the "aged sorrow," the inheritance of evil transmitted from generation to generation, an evil too intimately entwined with the complex conditions of society to be violently uprooted, but only to be gradually eradicated by the persistent cultivation of knowledge, industry, judgment, sobriety, and patience.

"This *is* only one example," she says, "of the law by which human lives are linked together; another example of what we complain of when we point to our pauperism, to the brutal ignorance of multitudes among our fellow-countrymen, to the weight of taxation laid on us by blamable wars, to the wasteful channels made for the public money, to the expense and trouble of getting justice, and call these the effects of bad rule. This is the law that we all bear the yoke of; the law of no man's making, and which no man can undo. Everybody now sees an example of it in the case of Ireland. We who are living now are sufferers by the wrong-doing of those who lived before us; we are sufferers by each other's wrong-doing; and the children who come after us will be sufferers from the same causes."

To remedy this long-standing wrong-doing and suffering, so argues Felix Holt, is not in the power of any one measure, class, or period. It would be childish folly to expect any Reform Bill to possess the magical property whereby a sudden social transformation could be accomplished. On the contrary, abrupt transitions should be shunned as dangerous to order and law, which alone are certain to insure a steady collective progress; the only means to this end consisting in the general spread of education, to

FELIX HOLT.

man should spare no pains. Without knowledge,
the writer continues, no political measures will be of
any benefit, ignorance with or without vote always
of necessity engendering vice and misery. But, guided
by a fuller knowledge, the working classes would
be able to discern what sort of men they should
choose for their representatives, and instead of elect-
ing "platform swaggerers, who bring us nothing but
the ocean to make our broth with," they would confide
the chief power to the hands of the truly wise, those
who know how to regulate life "according to the
truest principles mankind is in possession of."

The "Felix Holt" of the story is described by
George Eliot as shaping his actions much according
to the ideas which are here theoretically expressed.
His knowledge and aptitude would enable him to
choose what is considered a higher calling. But he
scorns the vulgar ambition called "getting on in the
world;" his sense of fellowship prompting him to
remain a simple artisan that he may exert an elevating
influence on the class to which he belongs. Class
differences, so argues this Radical-Conservative, being
inherent in the constitution of society, it becomes
something of a desertion to withdraw what abilities
one may have from the medium where they are
urgently needed, in order to join, for the sake of
selfish aims, some other body of men where they may
be superfluous.

The other distinctive feature of 'Felix Holt' consists in its elaborate construction, ranking it, so to
speak, amongst sensation novels. As a rule, George
Eliot's stories have little or no plot, the incidents
seeming not so much invented by the writer for the

N

sake of producing an effective work, as to be the
natural result of the friction between character and
circumstance. This simplicity of narrative belongs,
no doubt, to the highest class of novel, the class to
which 'The Vicar of Wakefield,' 'Waverley,' and
'Vanity Fair' belong. In 'Felix Holt,' however, the
intricate network of incident in which the characters
seem to be enmeshed, is not unlike the modern
French art of story-telling, with its fertility of invention, as is also the strangely repellent intrigue
which forms the nucleus of the whole. All the
elements which go to make up a thrilling narrative—
such as a dubious inheritance, the disappearance of
the rightful claimant, a wife's guilty secret, the involvements of the most desperate human fates in a
perplexing coil through sin and error—are interwoven
in this story of 'Felix Holt the Radical.'

Though ingeniously invented, the different incidents seem not so much naturally to have grown
the one from the other as to be constructed with
too conscious a seeking for effect. There is something forced, uneasy, and inadequate in the laborious contrivance of fitting one set of events on to
another, and the machinery of the disputed Transome claim is so involved that the reader never
masters the "ins" and "outs" of that baffling mystery.
Still, the groundwork of the story is deeply impressive: its interest is, notwithstanding the complex
ramification of events, concentrated with much power
upon a small group of personages, such as Mrs. Transome, her son Harold, the little dissenting minister,
Rufus Lyon, Esther, and Felix Holt. Here, as
elsewhere, the novelist reveals the potent qualities
of her genius. Not only does this story contain

such genuine humorous portraiture as the lachrymose Mrs. Holt, and the delightfully quaint Job Tudge, but it is also enriched by some descriptions of rural scenery and of homely existence in remote country districts as admirable as any to be found in her writings. Rufus Lyon is a worthy addition to that long gallery of clerical portraits which are among the triumphs of George Eliot's art. This "singular-looking apostle of the meeting in Skipper's Lane" —with his rare purity of heart, his unworldliness, his zeal in the cause of dissent, his restless argumentative spirit, and the moving memories of romance and passion hidden beneath the odd, quaint *physique* of the little minister encased in rusty black—is among the most loving and lovable of characters, and recalls more particularly that passage in the poem entitled 'A Minor Prophet,' which I cannot but think one of the author's finest, the passage beginning—

> " The pathos exquisite of lovely minds
> Hid in harsh forms—not penetrating them
> Like fire divine within a common bush
> Which glows transfigured by the heavenly guest,
> So that men put their shoes off; but encaged
> Like a sweet child within some thick-walled cell,
> Who leaps and fails to hold the window-bars,
> But having shown a little dimpled hand,
> Is visited thenceforth by tender hearts
> Whose eyes keep watch about the prison walls."

Esther, on the other hand, is one of those fortunate beings whose lovely mind is lodged in a form of corresponding loveliness. This charming Esther, though not originally without her feminine vanities and worldly desires, is one of those characters dear to

George Eliot's heart, who renounce the allurements
of an easy pleasurable existence for the higher satis-
factions of a noble love or a nobler ideal.   It is
curious to notice that Eppie, Esther, Fedalma, and
Daniel Deronda are all children that have been
reared in ignorance of their real parentage, and that
to all of them there comes a day when a more or
less difficult decision has to be made, when for good
or evil they have to choose, once for all, between
two conflicting claims.   Like Eppie, Esther rejects
the advantages of birth and fortune, and elects to
share the hard but dignified life of the high-minded
Felix.   But this decision in her case shows even
higher moral worth, because by nature she is so
keenly susceptible to the delicate refinements and
graceful elegancies which are the natural accompani-
ment of rank and wealth.

The most curious feature of this book consists,
perhaps, in its original treatment of illicit passion.
Novelists, as a rule, when handling this subject, depict
its fascinations in brilliant contrast to the sufferings
and terrors which follow in its train.   But George
Eliot contents herself with showing us the reverse
side of the medal.   Youth has faded, joy is dead, love
has turned to loathing, yet memory, like a relentless
fury, pursues the grey-haired Mrs. Transome, who
hides within her breast such a heavy load of shame
and dread.   The power and intensity with which this
character of the haughty, stern, yet inwardly quailing
woman is drawn are unsurpassed in their way, and
there is tragic horror in the recoil of her finest sensi-
bilities from the vulgar, mean, self-complacent lawyer,
too thick-skinned ever to know that in his own person
he is a daily judgment on her whose life has been

made hideous for his sake. Never more impressively than here does the novelist enforce her teaching that the deed follows the doer, being imbued with an incalculable vitality of its own, shaping all after life, and subduing to its guise the nature that is in bondage to it. Like those fabled dragon's teeth planted by Cadmus, which sprung up again as armed men, spreading discord and ruin, so a man's evil actions seem endowed with independent volition, and their consequences extend far beyond the individual life where they originated.

. If 'Felix Holt' is the most intricately constructed of George Eliot's novels, 'Middlemarch,' which appeared five years afterwards, is, on the other hand, a story without a plot. In fact, it seems hardly appropriate to call it a novel. Like Hogarth's serial pictures representing the successive stages in their progress through life of certain typical characters, so in this book there is unrolled before us, not so much the history of any particular individual, as a whole phase of society portrayed with as daring and uncompromising a fidelity to Nature as that of Hogarth himself. In 'Middlemarch,' English provincial life in the first half of the nineteenth century is indelibly fixed in words "holding a universe impalpable" for the apprehension and delight of the furthest generations of English-speaking nations. Here, as in some kind of panorama, sections of a community and groups of character pass before the mind's eye. To dwell on the separate, strongly-individualised figures which constitute this great crowd would be impossible within the present limits. But from the county people such as the Brookes and Chettams, to respectable middle-class families of the Vincy and Garth type, down to

the low, avaricious, harpy-tribes of the Waules and
Featherstones, every unit of this complex social agglo-
meration, is described with a life-like vividness truly
amazing, when the number and variety of the characters especially are considered. I know not where
else in literature to look for a work which leaves
such a strong impression on the reader's mind of
the intertexture of human lives. Seen thus in per-
spective, each separate individuality, with its special-
ised consciousness, is yet as indissolubly connected
with the collective life as that of the indistinguish-
able zoophyte which is but a sentient speck necessarily
moved by the same vital agency which stirs the entire
organism.

Among the figures which stand out most promi-
nently from the crowded background are Dorothea,
Lydgate, Casaubon, Rosamond Vincy, Ladislaw,
Bulstrode, Caleb, and Mary Garth. Dorothea belongs
to that stately type of womanhood, such as Romola
and Fedalma, a type which seems to be specifically
George Eliot's own, and which has perhaps more
in common with such Greek ideals as Antigone and
Iphigenia, than with more modern heroines. But
Dorothea, however lofty her aspirations, has not the
Christian heroism of Romola, or the antique devotion
of Fedalma. She is one of those problematic natures
already spoken of ; ill-adjusted to her circumstances,
and never quite adjusting circumstances to herself.
It is true that her high aims and glorious possibilities
are partially stifled by a social medium where there
seems no demand for them : still the resolute soul
usually finds some way in which to work out its
destiny.

"Many 'Theresas'" says George Eliot, "have

been born who found for themselves no epic life wherein there was a constant unfolding of far-resonant action; perhaps only a life of mistakes, the offspring of a certain spiritual grandeur ill-matched with the meanness of opportunity; perhaps a tragic failure which found no sacred poet, and sank unwept into oblivion. With dim lights and tangled circumstance they tried to shape their thought and deed in noble agreement; but, after all, to common eyes, their struggles seemed mere inconsistency and formlessness; for these later-born 'Theresas' were helped by no coherent social faith and order which could perform the function of knowledge for the ardently willing soul.

"Some have felt that these blundering lives are due to the inconvenient indefiniteness with which the Supreme Power has fashioned the natures of women; if there were one level of feminine incompetence as strict as the ability to count three and no more, the social lot of woman might be treated with scientific certitude. Meanwhile the indefiniteness remains, and the limits of variation are really much wider than any one would imagine from the sameness of women's coiffure, and the favourite love stories in prose and verse."

Such a life of mistakes is that of the beautiful Dorothea, the ill-starred wife of Casaubon. In his way the character of Casaubon is as great a triumph as that of Tito himself. The novelist seems to have crept into the inmost recesses of that uneasy consciousness, to have probed the most sensitive spots of that diseased vanity, and to lay bare before our eyes the dull labour of a brain whose ideas are stillborn. In an article by Mr. Myers it is stated, however incredible it may sound, that an undiscriminating friend once condoled with George Eliot on the melancholy experience which, from her knowledge of Lewes, had taught her to depict the gloomy character of Casaubon; whereas, in fact, there could not be a more striking contrast than that between the pedant groping amid dim fragments of knowledge, and the vivacious littérateur and thinker with his singular mental energy and grasp of thought. On the novelist's laughingly assuring him that such was by no means the case, "From whom, then," persisted he, "did you draw 'Casaubon'?" With a humorous solemnity, which was quite in earnest, she pointed to her own heart. She confessed, on the other hand, having found the character of Rosamond Vincy difficult to sustain, such complacency of egoism, as has been pointed out, being alien to her own habit of mind. But she laid no claim to any such natural magnanimity as could avert Casaubon's temptations of jealous vanity, and bitter resentment.

If there is any character in whom one may possibly trace some suggestions of Lewes, it is in the versatile, brilliant, talented Ladislaw, who held, that while genius must have the utmost play for its spontaneity, it may await with confidence "those messages from the universe which summon it to its peculiar work, only placing itself in an attitude of receptivity towards all sublime chances." But however charming, the impression Ladislaw produces is that of a somewhat shallow, frothy character, so that he seems almost as ill-fitted for Dorothea as the dreary Casaubon himself. Indeed the heroine's second marriage seems almost as much a failure as the stultifying union of Lydgate with Rosamond Vincy, and has altogether a more saddening effect than the tragic death of Maggie, which is how much less pitiful than that death in life of the fashionable doctor, whose best aims and vital purposes have been killed by his wife.

Much might be said of Bulstrode, the sanctimonious hypocrite, who is yet not altogether a hypocrite, but has a vein of something resembling goodness running through his crafty character; of Farebrother, the lax, amiable, genuinely honourable vicar of St. Botolph's; of Mrs. Cadwallader, the glib-tongued, witty, meddling rector's wife, a kind of Mrs. Poyser of high life; of Caleb Garth, whose devotion to work is a religion, and whose likeness to Mr. Robert Evans has already been pointed out; of the whole-hearted, sensible Mary, and of many other supremely vivid characters, whom to do justice to would carry us too far.

'Middlemarch' is the only work of George Eliot's, I believe, in which there is a distinct indication of her attitude towards the aspirations and clearly formulated demands of the women of the nineteenth century. Her many sarcastic allusions to the stereotyped theory about woman's sphere show on which side her sympathies were enlisted. On the whole, she was more partial to the educational movement than to that other agitation which aims at securing the political enfranchisement of women. How sincerely she had the first at heart is shown by the donation of 50*l.* "From the author of 'Romola,'" when Girton College was first started. And in a letter to a young lady who studied there, and in whose career she was much interested, she says, "the prosperity of Girton is very satisfactory." Among her most intimate friends, too, were some of the ladies who had initiated and organised the Women's Suffrage movement. Likewise writing to Miss Phelps, she alludes to the Woman's Lectureship in Boston, and remarks concerning the new University: "An office that may make a new precedent in social advance, and which is at the very least an experiment that ought to be tried. America is the seed-ground and nursery of new ideals, where they can grow in a larger, freer air than ours."

In 1871, the year when 'Middlemarch' was appearing in parts, George Eliot spent part of the spring and summer months at Shottermill, a quaint Hampshire village situated amid a landscape that unites beauties of the most varied kind. Here we may imagine her and Mr. Lewes, after their day's work was done, either seeking the vast stretch of heath and common only bounded by the horizon, or strolling through the deep-sunk lanes, or finding a soothing repose in "places of nestling green for poets made." They had rented Brookbank, an old-fashioned cottage with tiled roof and lattice-paned windows, belonging to Mrs. Gilchrist, the widow of the distinguished biographer of William Blake.

The description of Mrs. Meyrick's house in 'Daniel Deronda' "where the narrow spaces of wall held a world-history in scenes and heads," may have been suggested by her present abode, rich in original drawings by Blake, and valuable prints, and George Eliot writes: "If I ever steal anything in my life, I think it will be the two little Sir Joshuas over the drawing-room mantelpiece." At this time she and Mr. Lewes also found intense interest in reading the 'Life of Blake.' Some correspondence, kindly placed at my disposal by Mrs. Gilchrist, passed between this lady

and the Leweses in connection with the letting of the
house, giving interesting glimpses into the domesti-
cities of the latter. Their habits here, as in London,
were of clockwork regularity, household arrangements
being expected to run on wheels. "Everything," writes
George Eliot, "goes on slowly at Shottermill, and
the mode of narration is that typified in ' This is the
house that Jack built.' But there is an exquisite
stillness in the sunshine and a sense of distance from
London hurry, which encourages the growth of
patience.

"Mrs. G——'s " (their one servant) "pace is pro-
portionate to the other slownesses, but she impresses
me as a worthy person, and her cooking—indeed, all
her attendance on us—is of satisfactory quality. But
we find the awkwardness of having only one person in
the house, as well as the advantage (this latter being
quietude). The butcher does not bring the meat,
everybody grudges selling new milk, eggs are scarce,
and an expedition we made yesterday in search of
fowls, showed us nothing more hopeful than some
chickens six weeks old, which the good woman
observed were sometimes ' eaten by the gentry with
asparagus.' Those eccentric people, the gentry!

"But have we not been reading about the siege of
Paris all the winter, and shall we complain while we
get excellent bread and butter and many etceteras?
. . . Mrs S—— kindly sent us a dish of asparagus,
which we ate (without the skinny chicken) and had a
feast.

"You will imagine that we are as fond of eating as
Friar Tuck—I am enlarging so on our commissariat.
But you will also infer that we have no great evils to
complain of, since I make so much of the small."

George Eliot rarely went out in the day-time during her stay at Shottermill, but in the course of her rambles she would sometimes visit such cottagers in remote places as were not likely to know who she was. She used also to go and see a farmer's wife living at a short distance from Brookbank, with whom she would freely chat about the growth of fruits and vegetables and the quality of butter, much to the astonishment of the simple farm people. Speaking of her recollection of the great novelist to an American lady by whom these facts are recorded, the old countrywoman remarked : " It were wonderful, just wonderful, the sight o' green peas that I sent down to that gentleman and lady every week."

After the lapse of a few months spent in this sweet rural retreat, George Eliot again writes to Mrs. Gilchrist: "I did not imagine that I should ever be so fond of the place as I am now. The departure of the bitter winds, some improvement in my health, and the gradual revelation of fresh and fresh beauties in the scenery, especially under a hopeful sky such as we have sometimes had—all these conditions have made me love our little world here, and wish not to quit it until we can settle in our London home. I have the regret of thinking that it was my original indifference about it (I hardly ever like things until they are familiar) that hindered us from securing the cottage until the end of September."

George Eliot's conscientiousness and precision in the small affairs of life are exemplified in her last note to Mrs. Gilchrist: "After Mr. Lewes had written to you, I was made aware that a small dessert or bread-and-butter dish had been broken. That arch-sinner, the cat, was credited with the guilt. I am assured by

Mrs. G—— that nothing else has been injured during her reign, and Mrs. L—— confirmed the statement to me yesterday. I wish I could replace the unfortunate dish. . . . This note, of course, needs no answer, and it is intended simply to make me a clean breast about the crockery."

About this time George Eliot was very much out of health : indeed, both she and Lewes repeatedly speak of themselves as "two nervous, dyspeptic creatures, two ailing, susceptible bodies," to whom slight inconveniences are injurious and upsetting. Although it was hot summer weather, Mrs. Lewes suffered much from cold, sitting always with artificial heat to her feet. One broiling day in August, after she had left Brookbank, and taken another place in the neighbourhood, an acquaintance happening to call on her, found her sitting in the garden writing, as was her wont, her head merely shaded by a deodara, on the lawn. Being expostulated with by her visitor for her imprudence in exposing herself to the full blaze of the midday sun, she replied, "Oh, I like it! To-day is the first time I have felt warm this summer."

They led a most secluded life, George Eliot being at this time engaged with the continuation of 'Middlemarch ;' and Lewes, alluding to their solitary habits, writes at this date : "Work goes on smoothly away from all friendly interruptions. Lord Houghton says that it is incomprehensible how we can live in such Simeon Stylites fashion, as we often do, all alone—but the fact is we never *are* alone when alone. And I sometimes marvel how it is I have contrived to get through so much work living in London. It's true I'm a London child." Occasionally, however, they would

go and see Tennyson, whose house is only three miles
from Shottermill, but the road being all uphill made
the ride a little tedious and uncomfortable, especially
to George Eliot who had not got over her old nervous-
ness. The man who used to drive them on these
occasions was so much struck by this that he told the
lady who has recorded these details in the *Century
Magazine:* "Withal her being such a mighty clever
body, she were very nervous in a carriage—allays
wanted to go on a smooth road, and seemed dreadful
feared of being thrown out." On one of these occasional meetings with Tennyson, the poet got involved
in a conversation with the novelist concerning evolution and such weighty questions. They had been
walking together in close argument, and as the Poet-
Laureate bade George Eliot farewell, he called to her,
already making her way down the hill, "Well, good-
by, you and your molecules!" And she, looking back,
said in her deep low voice (which always got lower
when she was at all roused), "I am quite content with
my molecules."

The country all around Shottermill with its breezy
uplands, its pine-clad hills, its undulating tracts of
land purpled with heath in the autumn, became more
and more endeared to George Eliot, who, indeed, liked
it better than any scenery in England. Here she
could enjoy to the full that "sense of standing on a
round world," which, she writes to Mrs. Gilchrist
who had used the phrase, "was precisely what
she most cared for amongst out-of-door delights."
Some years afterwards we find her and Mr. Lewes
permanently taking a house not far off, at Witley in
Surrey, which has the same kind of beautiful open
scenery. Writing from her town residence about it to

her old friend Mrs. Bray, George Eliot says : " We, too, are thinking of a new settling down, for we have bought a house in Surrey about four miles from God-alming on a gravelly hill among the pine-trees, but with neighbours to give us a sense of security. Our present idea is that we shall part with this house and give up London except for occasional visits. We shall be on the same line of railway with some good friends at Weybridge and Guildford."

CHAPTER XIV.

DANIEL DERONDA.

'DANIEL DERONDA,' which appeared five years after 'Middlemarch,' occupies a place apart among George Eliot's novels. In the spirit which animates it, it has perhaps the closest affinity with the 'Spanish Gypsy.' Speaking of this work to a young friend of Jewish extraction (in whose career George Eliot felt keen interest), she expressed surprise at the amazement which her choice of a subject had created. "I wrote about the Jews," she remarked, "because I consider them a fine old race who have done great things for humanity. I feel the same admiration for them as I do for the Florentines. Only lately I have heard to my great satisfaction that an influential member of the Jewish community is going to start an emigration to Palestine. You will also be glad to learn that Helmholtz is a Jew."

These observations are valuable as affording a key to the leading motive of 'Daniel Deronda.' Mordecai's ardent desire to found a new national state in Palestine is not simply the author's dramatic realisation of the feeling of an enthusiast, but expresses her own very definite sentiments on the subject. The Jewish apostle is, in fact, more or less the mouthpiece of George Eliot's own opinions on Judaism. For so great a master in the art of creating character, this type of the loftiest kind of man is curiously unreal. Mordecai delivers himself of the most eloquent and exalted views and sentiments, yet his own personality remains so vague and nebulous that it has no power of kindling the imagination. Mordecai is meant for a Jewish Mazzini. Within his consciousness he harbours the future of a people. He feels himself destined to become the saviour of his race; yet he does not convince us of his greatness. He convinces us no more than he does the mixed company at the "Hand and Banner," which listens with pitying incredulity to his passionate harangues. Nevertheless the first and final test of the religious teacher or of the social reformer is the magnetic force with which his own intense beliefs become binding on the consciences of others, if only of a few. It is true Mordecai secures one disciple — the man destined to translate his thought into action, Daniel Deronda, as shadowy, as puppet-like, as lifeless as Ezra Mordecai Cohen himself. These two men, of whom the one is the spiritual leader and the other the hero destined to realise his aspirations, are probably the two most unsuccessful of George Eliot's vast gallery of characters. They are the representatives of an idea, but the idea has never been made flesh. A succinct expression of it may be gathered from the following passage :

" Which among the chief of the Gentile nations has not an ignorant multitude? They scorn our people's ignorant observance ; but the most accursed ignorance is that which has no observance—sunk to the cunning greed of the fox, to which all law is no more than a trap or the cry of the worrying hound. There is a

degradation deep down below the memory that has
withered into superstition.   For the multitude of the
ignorant on three continents who observe our rites and
make the confession of the Divine Unity the Lord of
Judaism is not dead.   Revive the organic centre : let
the unity of Israel which has made the growth and
form of its religion be an outward reality.   Looking
towards a land and a polity, our dispersed people in
all the ends of the earth may share the dignity of
a national life which has a voice among the peoples of
the East and the West ; which will plant the wisdom
and skill of our race, so that it may be, as of old, a
medium of transmission and understanding.   Let that
come to pass, and the living warmth will spread to the
weak extremities of Israel, and superstition will vanish,
not in the lawlessness of the renegade, but in the
illumination of great facts which widen feeling, and
make all knowledge alive as the young offspring of
beloved memories."

 This notion that the Jews should return to Palestine
in a body, and once more constitute themselves into a
distinct nation, is curiously repugnant to modern feelings.   As repugnant as that other doctrine, which is
also implied in the book, that Jewish separateness
should be still further insured by strictly adhering to
their own race in marriage—at least Mirah, the most
faultless of George Eliot's heroines, whose character
expresses the noblest side of Judaism, "is a Jewess
who will not accept any one but a Jew."

 Mirah Lapidoth and the Princess Halm-Eberstein,
Deronda's mother, are drawn with the obvious purpose of contrasting two types of Jewish women.
Whereas the latter, strictly brought up in the belief
and most minute observances of her Hebrew father,

breaks away from the "bondage of having been born a Jew," from which she wishes to relieve her son by parting from him in infancy, Mirah, brought up in disregard, "even in dislike of her Jewish origin," clings with inviolable tenacity to the memory of that origin and to the fellowship of her people. The author leaves one in little doubt as towards which side her own sympathies incline to. She is not so much the artist here, impartially portraying different kinds of characters, as the special pleader proclaiming that one set of motives are righteous, just, and praiseworthy, as well as that the others are mischievous and reprehensible.

This seems carrying the principle of nationality to an extreme, if not pernicious length. If there were never any breaking up of old forms of society, any fresh blending of nationalities and races, we should soon reduce Europe to another China. This unwavering faithfulness to the traditions of the past may become a curse to the living. A rigidity as unnatural as it is dangerous would be the result of too tenacious a clinging to inherited memories. For if this doctrine were strictly carried out, such a country as America, where there is a slow amalgamation of many allied and even heterogeneous races into a new nation, would practically become impossible. Indeed, George Eliot does not absolutely hold these views. She considers them necessary at present in order to act as a drag to the too rapid transformations of society. In the most interesting paper of 'Theophrastus Such,' that called 'The Modern Hep! Hep! Hep!' she remarks: "The tendency of things is towards quicker or slower fusion of races. It is impossible to arrest this tendency; all we can do is to moderate its course

so as to hinder it from degrading the moral status of
societies by a too rapid effacement of those national
traditions and customs which are the language of the
national genius—the deep suckers of healthy sentiment. Such moderating and guidance of inevitable
movement is worthy of all effort."

Considering that George Eliot was convinced of
this modern tendency towards fusion, it is all the
more singular that she should, in 'Daniel Deronda,'
have laid such stress on the reconstruction, after the
lapse of centuries, of a Jewish state ; singular, when
one considers that many of the most eminent Jews,
far from aspiring towards such an event, hardly seem
to have contemplated it as a desirable or possible prospect. The sympathies of Spinoza, the Mendelssohns,
Rahel, Meyerbeer, Heine, and many others, are
not distinctively Jewish but humanitarian. And the
grandest, as well as truest thing that has been uttered
about them is that saying of Heine's : "The country
of the Jews is the ideal, is God."

Indeed, to have a true conception of Jewish nature
and character, of its brilliant lights and deep shadows,
of its pathos, depth, sublimity, degradation, and wit ;
of its infinite resource and boundless capacity for
suffering—one must go to Heine and not to 'Daniel
Deronda.' In 'Jehuda-ben-Halevy' Heine expresses
the love and longing of a Jewish heart for Jerusalem
in accents of such piercing intensity that compared
with it, "Mordecai's" fervid desire fades into mere
abstract rhetoric.

Nature and experience were the principal sources
of George Eliot's inspiration. And though she knew
a great deal about the Jews, her experience had not
become sufficiently incorporated with her conscious-

ness. Otherwise, instead of portraying such tame models of perfection as Deronda and Mirah, she would have so mixed her colours as to give us that subtle involvement of motive and tendency—as of cross-currents in the sea—which we find in the characters of nature's making and in her own finest creations, such as Maggie, Silas Marner, Dorothea Casaubon, and others.

In turning to the English portion of the story there is at once greater play of spontaneity in the people depicted. Grandcourt, Gascoigne, Rex, Mrs. Davilow, Sir Hugh Mallinger, and especially Gwendolen, show all the old cunning in the psychological rendering of human nature. Curiously enough, this novel consists of two perfectly distinct narratives ; the only point of junction being Daniel Deronda himself, who, as a Jew by birth and an English gentleman by education, stands related to both sets of circumstances. The influence he exerts on the spiritual development of Gwendolen seems indeed the true *motif* of the story. Otherwise there is no intrinsic connection between the group of people clustering round Mordecai, and that of which Gwendolen is the centre : unless it be that the author wished to show the greater intensity of aim and higher moral worth of the Jews as contrasted with these purposeless, worldly, unideal Christians of the nineteenth century.

Compared with the immaculate Mirah, Gwendolen Harleth is a very naughty, spoiled, imperfect speci- men of maidenhood. But she has life in her ; and one speculates as to what she will say and do next, as if she were a person among one's acquaintances. On that account most readers of ' Daniel Deronda ' find their

interest engrossed by the fate of Gwendolen, and the
conjugal relations between her and Grandcourt. This
is so much the case, that one suspects her to have
been the first idea of the story. She is at any rate
its most attractive feature. In Gwendolen, George
Eliot once remarked, she had wished to draw a girl of
the period. Fascinating, accomplished, of siren-like
beauty, she has every outward grace combined
with a singular inward vacuity. The deeper aspects
of life are undreamed of in her philosophy. Her
religion consists in a vague awe of the unknown and
invisible, and her ambition in the acquisition of rank,
wealth, and personal distinction. She is selfish, vain,
frivolous, worldly, domineering, yet not without
sudden impulses of generosity, and jets of affection.
Something there is in her of Undine before she had
a soul—something of a gay, vivacious, unfeeling
sprite, who recks nothing of human love or of human
misery, but looks down with utter indifference on the
poor humdrum mortals around her, whom she inspires
at once with fear and fondness: something, also, of
the "princess in exile, who in time of famine was to
have her breakfast-roll made of the finest bolted flour
from the seven thin ears of wheat, and in a general
decampment was to have her silver fork kept out of
the baggage."

How this bewitching creature, whose "iridescence
of character" makes her a psychological problem, is
gradually brought to accept Henleigh Grandcourt,
in spite of the promise she has given to Lydia
Glasher (his discarded victim), and her own fleeting
presentiments, is described with an analytical subtlety
unsurpassed in George Eliot's works. So, indeed, is
the whole episode of the married life of Grandcourt.

This territorial magnate, who possesses every worldly advantage that Gwendolen desired, is worthy, as a study of character, to be placed beside that of Casaubon himself. Gwendolen's girlish type of egoism, which loves to be the centre of admiration, here meets with that far other deadlier form of an "exorbitant egoism," conspicuous for its intense obstinacy and tenacity of rule, "in proportion as the varied susceptibilities of younger years are stripped away." This cold, negative nature lies with a kind of withering blight on the susceptible Gwendolen. Roused from the complacent dreams of girlhood by the realities of her married life, shrinking in helpless repulsion from the husband whom she meant to manage, and who holds her as in a vice, the unhappy woman has nothing to cling to in this terrible inward collapse of her happiness, but the man, who, from the first moment when his eye arrests hers at the gaming table at Leubronn, becomes, as it were, a conscience visibly incarnate to her. This incident, which is told in the first chapter of the novel, recalls a sketch by Dante Rossetti, where Mary Magdalene, in the flush of joyous life, is held by the Saviour's gaze, and in a sudden revulsion from her old life, breaks away from companions that would fain hold her back, with a passionate movement towards the Man of Sorrow. This impressive conception may have unconsciously suggested a somewhat similar situation to the novelist, for that George Eliot was acquainted with this drawing is shown by the following letter addressed in 1870 to Dante Rossetti:

"I have had time now to dwell on the photographs. I am especially grateful to you for giving me the head marked June 1861 : it is exquisite. But I am glad

to possess every one of them. The subject of the
Magdalene rises in interest for me, the more I look
at it. I hope you will keep in the picture an equally
passionate type for her. Perhaps you will indulge
me with a little talk about the modifications you
intend to introduce."

The relation of Deronda to Gwendolen is of a
Christlike nature. He is her only moral hold in
the fearful temptations that assail her now and
again under the intolerable irritations of her married
life, temptations which grow more urgent when
Grandcourt leads his wife captive, after his fashion,
in a yacht on the Mediterranean. For "the intensest
form of hatred is that rooted in fear, which compels
to silence, and drives vehemence into a constructive
vindictiveness, an imaginary annihilation of the de-
tested object, something like the hidden rites of
vengeance, with which the persecuted have made
a dark vent for their rage, and soothed their suffering
nto dumbness. Such hidden rites went on in the
secrecy of Gwendolen's mind, but not with soothing
effect—rather with the effect of a struggling terror.
Side by side with dread of her husband had grown
the self-dread which urged her to flee from the pursuing images wrought by her pent-up impulse."

The evil wish at last finds fulfilment, the murderous
thought is outwardly realised. And though death is
not eventually the result of the criminal desire, it yet
seems to the unhappy wife as if it had a determining
power in bringing about the catastrophe. But it is
precisely this remorse which is the redeeming quality
of her nature, and awakens a new life within her. In
this quickening of the moral consciousness through
guilt we are reminded, although in a different man-

ner, of a similar process, full of pregnant suggestions, described in Nathaniel Hawthorne's 'Transformation.' It will be remembered that Donatello leads a purely instinctive, that is to say animal, existence, till the commission of a crime awakens the dormant conscience, and a soul is born in the throes of anguish and remorse.

In 'Daniel Deronda' there is an entire absence of that rich, genial humour which seemed spontaneously to bubble up and overflow her earlier works. Whether George Eliot's conception of the Jews as a peculiarly serious race had any share in bringing about that result, it is difficult to say. At any rate, in one of her essays she remarks that, "The history and literature of the ancient Hebrews gives the idea of a people who went about their business and pleasure as gravely as a society of beavers." Certainly Mordecai, Deronda, and Mirah, are preternaturally solemn; even the Cohen family are not presented with any of those comic touches one would have looked for in this great humorist: only in the boy Jacob are there gleams of drollery, such as in this description of him by Hans Meyrick: "He treats me with the easiest familiarity, and seems in general to look at me as a second-hand Christian commodity, likely to come down in price; remarking on my disadvantages with a frankness which seems to imply some thoughts of future purchase. It is pretty, though, to see the change in him if Mirah happens to come in. He turns child suddenly—his age usually strikes one as being like the Israelitish garments in the desert, perhaps near forty, yet with an air of recent production."

A certain subdued vein of humour is not entirely absent from the portraiture of the Meyrick family, a delightful group, who "had their little oddities, streaks of eccentricity from the mother's blood as well as the father's, their minds being like mediæval houses with unexpected recesses and openings from this into that, flights of steps, and sudden outlooks." But on the whole, instead of the old humour, we find in 'Daniel Deronda' a polished irony and epigrammatic sarcasm, which were afterwards still more fully developed in the 'Impressions of Theophrastus Such.'

Soon after the publication of this novel, we find the following allusion to it in one of George Eliot's letters to Mrs. Bray : "I don't know what you refer to in the *Jewish World.*--Perhaps the report of Dr. Hermann Adler's lecture on 'Deronda' to the Jewish working-men, given in the *Times.* Probably the Dr. Adler whom you saw is Dr. Hermann's father, still living as Chief-Rabbi. I have had some delightful communications from Jews and Jewesses, both at home and abroad. Part of the Club scene in 'D. D.' is flying about in the Hebrew tongue through the various Hebrew newspapers, which have been copying the 'Maga.' in which the translation was first sent to me three months ago. The Jews naturally are not indifferent to themselves."

This Club scene gave rise at the time to quite a controversy. It could not fail to be identified with that other club of philosophers out at elbows so vividly described by G. H. Lewes in the 'Fortnightly Review' of 1866. Nor was it possible not to detect an affinity between the Jew Cohen, the poor consumptive journeyman watchmaker, with his weak voice and his great calm intellect, and Ezra Mordecai Cohen, in precisely similar conditions ; the difference being that the one is penetrated by the philosophical idea of

Spinozism, and the other by the political idea of reconstituting a Jewish State in Palestine. This difference of mental bias, no doubt, forms a contrast between the two characters, without, however, invalidating the surmise that the fictitious enthusiast may have been originally suggested by the noble figure of the living Jew. Be that as it may, Lewes often took the opportunity in conversation of "pointing out that no such resemblance existed, Cohen being a keen dialectician and a highly impressive man, but without any specifically Jewish enthusiasm."

When she undertook to write about the Jews, George Eliot was deeply versed in Hebrew literature, ancient and modern. She had taught herself Hebrew when translating the *Leben Jesu*, and this knowledge now stood her in good stead. She was also familiar with the splendid utterances of Jehuda-ben-Halevy; with the visionary speculations of the Cabbalists, and with the brilliant Jewish writers of the Hispano-Arabic epoch. She had read portions of the Talmud, and remarked one day in conversation that Spinoza had really got something from the Cabbala. On her friend humbly suggesting that by ordinary accounts it appeared to be awful nonsense, she said "that it nevertheless contained fine ideas, like Plato and the Old Testament, which, however, people took in the lump, being accustomed to them."

CHAPTER XV.

LAST YEARS.

'DANIEL DERONDA' is the last great imaginative work with which George Eliot was destined to enrich the world. It came out in small volumes, the appearance of each fresh number being hailed as a literary event. In allusion to an author's feeling on the conclusion of a weighty task, George Eliot remarks in one of her letters: "As to the great novel which remains to be written, I must tell you that I never believe in future books. . . . Always after finishing a book ·I have a period of despair that I can never again produce anything worth giving to the world. The responsibility of the writer grows heavier and heavier—does it not?—as the world grows older, and the voices of the dead more numerous. It is difficult to believe, until the germ of some new work grows into imperious activity within one, that it is possible to make a really needed contribution to the poetry of the world—I mean possible to oneself to do it."

This singular diffidence, arising from a sense of the tremendous responsibility which her position entailed, was one of the most noticeable characteristics of this great woman, and struck every one who came in contact with her. Her conscientiousness made her even painfully anxious to enter sympathetically into the needs of every person who approached her, so as to make her speech a permanently fruitful influence in her hearer's life. Such an interview, for example, as that between Goethe and Heine—where the younger poet, after thinking all the way what fine things to say to Goethe, was so disconcerted by the awe-inspiring presence of the master, that he could find nothing better to say than that the plums on the road-side between Jena and Weimar were remarkably good—would have been impossible with one so eager always to give of her best.

This deep seriousness of nature made her Sunday afternoon receptions, which became more and more fashionable as time went on, something of a tax to one who preferred the intimate converse of a few to that more superficially brilliant talk which a promiscuous gathering brings with it. Among the distinguished visitors to be met more or less frequently at the Priory may be mentioned Mr. Herbert Spencer, Professor Huxley, Mr. Frederic Harrison, Professor Beesly, Dr. and Mrs. Congreve, Madame Bodichon, Lord Houghton, M. Tourguénief, Mr. Ralston, Sir Theodore and Lady Martin (better known as Helen Faucit), Mr. Burton of the National Gallery, Mr. George Howard and his wife, Mr. C. G. Leland, Mr. Moncure Conway, Mr. Justin McCarthy, Dr. Hueffer, Mr. and Mrs. Buxton Forman, Mr. F. Myers, Mr. Sully, Mr. Du Maurier, Mr. and Mrs. Mark Pattison, Mr. and Mrs. W. K. Clifford, Lady Castletown and her daughters, Mr. and Mrs. Burne Jones, Mr. John Everett Millais, Mr. Robert Browning, and Mr. Tennyson.

Persons of celebrity were not the only ones, however, that were made welcome at the Priory. The

liveliest sympathy was shown by both host and
hostess in many young people as yet struggling in
obscurity, but in whom they delighted to recognise
the promise of some future excellence.   If a young
man were pursuing some original scientific inquiry,
or striking out a new vein of speculation, in all London
there was none likely to enter with such zest into his
ideas as G. H. Lewes.   His generous appreciation of
intellectual gifts' is well shown in the following lines
to the late Mr. W. K. Clifford :

"Few things have given us more pleasure than the
intimation in your note that you had a *fiancée*.   May
she be the central happiness and motive force of your
career, and, by satisfying the affections, leave your
rare intellect free to work out its glorious destiny.   For,
if you don't become a glory to your age and time, it
will be a sin and a shame.   Nature doesn't often
send forth such gifted sons, and when she does,
Society usually cripples them.   Nothing but marriage
—a happy marriage—has seemed to Mrs. Lewes and
myself wanting to your future."

On the Sunday afternoon receptions just mentioned,
G. H. Lewes acted, so to speak, as a social cement.
His vivacity, his ready tact, the fascination of his
manners, diffused that general sense of ease and
abandon so requisite to foster an harmonious flow of
conversation.   He was inimitable as a *raconteur*, and
Thackeray, Trollope, and Arthur Helps were fond of
quoting some of the stories which he would dramatise
in the telling.   One of the images which, on these
occasions, recurs oftenest to George Eliot's friends,
is that of the frail-looking woman who would sit with
her chair drawn close to the fire, and whose winning
womanliness of bearing and manners struck every one

who had the privilege of an introduction to her. Her long, pale face, with its strongly-marked features, was less rugged in the mature prime of life than in youth, the inner meanings of her nature having worked themselves more and more to the surface, the mouth, with its benignant suavity of expression, especially softening the too prominent under-lip and massive jaw. Her abundant hair, untinged with grey, whose smooth bands made a kind of frame to the face, was covered by a lace or muslin cap, with lappets of rich point or Valenciennes lace fastened under her chin. Her grey-blue eyes, under noticeable eyelashes, expressed the same acute sensitiveness as her long, thin, beautifully-shaped hands. She had a pleasant laugh and smile, her voice being low, distinct, and intensely sympathetic in quality : it was contralto in singing, but she seldom sang or played before more than one or two friends. Though her conversation was perfectly easy, each sentence was as finished, as perfectly formed, as the style of her published works. Indeed, she laid great stress on the value of correct speaking and clearness of enunciation ; and in 'Theophrastus Such' she laments "the general ambition to speak every language except our mother English, which persons 'of style' are not ashamed of corrupting with slang, false foreign equivalents, and a pronunciation that crushes out all colour from the vowels, and jams them between jostling consonants."

Besides M. d'Albert's Genevese portrait of George Eliot, we have a drawing by Mr. Burton, and another by Mr. Lawrence, the latter taken soon after the publication of 'Adam Bede.' In criticising the latter likeness, a keen observer of human nature remarked that it conveyed no indication of the infinite depth of her observant eye, nor of that cold, subtle, and unconscious cruelty of expression which might occasionally be detected there. George Eliot had an unconquerable aversion to her likeness being taken: once, however, in 1860, she was photographed for the sake of her "dear sisters" at Rosehill. But she seems to have repented of this weakness, for, after the lapse of years, she writes : "Mr. Lewes has just come to me after reading your letter, and says, 'For God's sake tell her not to have the photograph reproduced!' and I had nearly forgotten to say that the fading is what I desired. I should not like this image to be perpetuated. It needs the friendly eyes that regret to see it fade, and must not be recalled into emphatic black and white for indifferent gazers. Pray let it vanish."

Those who knew George Eliot were even more struck by the force of her entire personality than by her writings. Sympathetic, witty or learned in turn, her conversation deeply impressed her hearers, being enriched by such felicities of expression as : "The best lesson of tolerance we have to learn is to tolerate intolerance." In answer to a friend's surprise that a clever man should allow himself to be contradicted by a stupid one, without dropping down on him, she remarked : "He is very liable to drop down as a baked apple would." And of a very plain acquaintance she said : "He has the most dreadful kind of ugliness one can be afflicted with, because it takes on the semblance of beauty."

Poetry, music, and art naturally absorbed much attention at the Priory. Here Mr. Tennyson has been known to read 'Maud' aloud to his friends : Mr. Browning expatiated on the most recondite metrical rules : and Rossetti sent presents of poems and photographs. In the following unpublished letters George Eliot thanks the latter for his valued gifts—"We returned only the night before last from a two months' journey to the Continent, and among the parcels awaiting me I found your generous gift. I am very grateful to you both as giver and poet.

"In cutting the leaves, while my head is still swimming from the journey, I have not resisted the temptation to read many things as they ought not to be read—hurriedly. But even in this way I have received a stronger impression than any fresh poems have for a long while given me, that to read once is a reason for reading again. The sonnets towards 'The House of Life' attract me peculiarly. I feel about them as I do about a new cahier of music which I have been 'trying' here and there with the delightful conviction that I have a great deal to become acquainted with and to like better and better." And again, in acknowledgment of some photographs: "The 'Hamlet' seems to me perfectly intelligible, and altogether admirable in conception, except in the type of the man's head. I feel sure that 'Hamlet' had a square anterior lobe.

"Mr. Lewes says, this conception of yours makes him long to be an actor who has 'Hamlet' for one of his parts, that he might carry out this scene according to your idea.

"One is always liable to mistake prejudices for sufficient inductions, about types of head and face, as well as about all other things. I have some impressions—perhaps only prejudices dependent on the narrowness of my experience—about forms of eyebrow and their relation to passionate expression. It is possible that such a supposed relation has a real anatomical basis.

But in many particulars facial expression is like the expression of hand-writing : the relations are too subtle and intricate to be detected, and only shallowness is confident."

George Eliot read but little contemporary fiction, being usually absorbed in the study of some particular subject. "For my own spiritual good I need all other sort of reading," she says, "more than I need fiction. I know nothing of contemporary English novelists with the exception of ——, and a few of ——'s works. My constant groan is that I must leave so much of the greatest writing which the centuries have sifted for me unread for want of time." For the same reason, on being recommended by a literary friend to read Walt Whitman, she hesitated on the ground of his not containing anything spiritually needful for her, but, having been induced to take him up, she changed her opinion and admitted that he *did* contain what was "good for her soul." As to lighter reading, she was fond of books of travel, pronouncing "'The Voyage of the Challenger' a splendid book." Among foreign novelists she was very partial to Henry Gréville, and speaks of 'Les Koumiassine' as a pleasant story.

Persons who were privileged enough to be admitted to the intimacy of George Eliot and Mr. Lewes could not fail to be impressed by the immense admiration which they had for one another. Lewes's tenderness, always on the watch lest the great writer, with her delicately poised health, should over-exert herself, had something of doglike fidelity. On the other hand, in spite of George Eliot's habitually retiring manner, if any one ever engaged on the opposite side of an argument to that maintained by the brilliant *savant,* in taking his part, she usually had the best of it, although in the most gentle and feminine way.

Although there was entire oneness of feeling between them, there was no unanimity of opinion. George Eliot had the highest regard for Lewes's opinions, but held to her own. One of the chief subjects of difference consisted in their attitude towards Christianity ; whereas he was its uncompromising opponent, she had the greatest sympathy with its various manifestations from Roman Catholic asceticism to Evangelical austerity and Methodist fervour. Her reverence for every form of worship in which mankind has more or less consciously embodied its sense of the mystery of all "this unintelligible world" increased with the years. She was deeply penetrated by that tendency of the Positivist spirit which recognises the beneficial element in every form of religion, and sees the close, nay indissoluble, connection between the faith of former generations and the ideal of our own. She herself found ample scope for the needs and aspirations of her spiritual nature in the religion of humanity. As has already been repeatedly pointed out, there runs through all her works the same persistent teaching of "the Infinite Nature of Duty." And with Comte she refers "the obligations of duty, as well as all sentiments of devotion, to a concrete object, at once ideal and real ; the Human Race, conceived as a continuous whole, including the past, the present, and the future."

Though George Eliot drew many of her ideas of moral cultivation from the doctrines of Comte's *Philosophie Positive,* she was not a Positivist in the strict sense of the word. Her mind was far too creative by nature to give an unqualified adhesion to such a system as Comte's. Indeed, her devotion to the idea of mankind, conceived as a collective whole, is not so much characteristic of Positivists as of the greatest modern minds, minds such as Lessing, Bentham, Shelley, Mill, Mazzini, and Victor Hugo. Inasmuch as Comte co-ordinated these ideas into a consistent doctrine, George Eliot found herself greatly attracted to his system; and~Mr. Beesly, after an acquaintance of eighteen years, considered himself justified in stating that her powerful intellect had accepted the teaching of Auguste Comte, and that she looked forward to the reorganisation of belief on the lines which he had laid down. Still her adherence, like that of G. H. Lewes, was only partial, and applied mainly to his philosophy, and not to his scheme of social policy. She went farther than the latter, however, in her concurrence. For Mr. Lewes, speaking of the *Politique Positive* in his 'History of Philosophy,' admits that his antagonistic attitude had been considerably modified on learning from the remark of one very dear to him, "to regard it as an Utopia, presenting hypotheses rather than doctrines—suggestions for future inquiries rather than dogmas for adepts."

On the whole, although George Eliot did not agree with Comte's later theories concerning the reconstruction of society, she regarded them with sympathy "as the efforts of an individual to anticipate the work of future generations." This sympathy with the general Positivist movement she showed by subscribing regularly to Positivist objects, especially to the fund of the Central Organisation presided over by M. Laffitte, but she invariably refused all membership with the

Positivist community. In conversation with an old and valued friend, she also repeatedly expressed her objection to much in Comte's later speculations, saying on one occasion, " I cannot submit my intellect or my soul to the guidance of Comte." The fact is that, although George Eliot was greatly influenced by the leading Positivist ideas, her mind was too original not to work out her own individual conception of life.

What this conception is has been already indicated, so far as space would permit, in the discussion of her successive works. Perhaps in the course of time her moralising analytical tendency encroached too much on the purely artistic faculty. Her eminently dramatic genius—which enabled her to realise characters the most varied and opposite in type, somewhat in the manner of Shakespeare—became hampered by theories and abstract views of life. This was especially shown in her latest work, 'The Impressions of Theophrastus Such,' a series of essays chiefly satirising the weaknesses and vanities of the literary class. In these unattractive "impressions" the wit is often laboured, and does not play "beneficently round the changing facets of egoism, absurdity, and vice, as the sunshine over the rippling sea or the dewy meadows." Its cutting irony and incisive ridicule are no longer tempered by the humorous laugh, but have the corrosive quality of some acrid chemical substance.

One of the papers, however, that entitled ' Debasing the Moral Currency,' expresses a strongly marked characteristic of George Eliot's mind. It is a pithy protest against the tendency of the present generation to turn the grandest deeds and noblest works of art into food for laughter. For she hated nothing so much as mockery and ridicule of what other peo{ reverenced, often remarking that those who considered themselves freest from superstitious fancies were the most intolerant. She carried this feeling to such a pitch that she even disliked a book like 'Alice in Wonderland' because it laughed at the things which children had had a kind of belief in. In censuring this vicious habit of burlesquing the things that ought to be regarded with awe and admiration, she remarks, "Let a greedy buffoonery debase all historic beauty, majesty and pathos, and the more you heap up the desecrated symbols, the greater will be the lack of the ennobling emotions which subdue the tyranny of suffering, and make ambition one with virtue."

'Looking Backward' is the only paper in 'Theophrastus Such' quite free from cynicism. It contains, under a slightly veiled form, pathetically tender reminiscences of her own early life. This volume, not published till May 1879, was written before the incalculable loss which befell George Eliot in the autumn of the preceding year.

After spending the summer of 1878 in the pleasant retirement of Witley, Lewes and George Eliot returned to London. A severe cold taken by Lewes proved the forerunner of a serious disorder, and, after a short illness, this bright, many-sided, indefatigable thinker, passed away in his sixty-second year. He had frequently said to his friends that the most desirable end of a well-spent life was a painless death; and although his own could not be called painless, his sufferings were at least of short duration. Concerning the suffering and anguish of her who was left behind to mourn him, one may most fitly say, in her own words, that, "for the first sharp pangs there is no comfort — whatever goodness may surround us, darkness and silence still hang about our pain." In her case, also, the "clinging companionship with the dead" was gradually linked with her living affections, and she found alleviation for her sorrow in resuming those habits of continuous mental occupation which had become second nature with her. In a letter addressed to a friend, who, only a few short months afterwards, suffered a like heavy bereavement, there breathes the spirit in which George Eliot bore her own sorrow: "I understand it all. . . . There is but one refuge—the having much to do. You have the mother's duties. Not that these can yet make your life other than a burden to be patiently borne. Nothing can, except the gradual adaptation of your soul to the new conditions. . . . It is among my most cherished memories that I knew your husband, and from the first delighted in him. . . . All blessing—and even the sorrow that is a form of love has a heart of blessing—is tenderly wished for you."

On seeing this lady for the first time after their mutual loss, George Eliot asked her eagerly: "Do the children help? Does it make any difference?" Some help there was for the widowed heart of this sorrowing woman in throwing herself, with all her energies, into the work which Lewes had left unfinished at his death, and preparing it for publication, with the help of an expert. Another subject which occupied her thoughts at this time, was the foundation of the "George Henry Lewes Studentship," in order to commemorate the name of one who had done so much to distinguish himself in the varied fields of literature, science, and philosophy. The value of the studentship is slightly under £200 a year.

It is worth noticing that persons of both sexes are received as candidates. The object of the endowment is to encourage the prosecution of original research in physiology, a science to whose study Lewes had devoted himself most assiduously for many years. Writing of this matter to a young lady, one of the Girton students, George Eliot says : " I know . . . will be glad to hear also that both in England and Germany the type, or scheme, on which the studentship is arranged has been regarded with satisfaction, as likely to be a useful model."

Amid such preoccupations, and the preparation of 'Theophrastus Such' for the press, the months passed on, and George Eliot was beginning to see her friends again, when one day she not only took the world, but her intimate circle by surprise, by her marriage with Mr. John Walter Cross, on the 6th of May, 1880. The acquaintance with this gentleman, dating from the year 1867, had long ago grown into the warmest friendship, and his boundless devotion to the great woman whose society was to him as his daily bread, no doubt induced her to take a step which could not fail to startle even those who loved her the most. But George Eliot's was a nature that needed some one especially to love. And though that precious companionship, at once stimulating and sympathetic, which she had so long enjoyed, was taken from her, she could still find comfort during the remainder of her life in the love, the appreciation, and the tender care which were proffered to her by Mr. Cross. Unfortunately her life was not destined to be prolonged.

Although seeming fairly well at this date, George Eliot's health, always delicate, had probably received a shock, from which it never recovered. Only six months before her marriage three eminent medical men were attending her for a painful disease. However, there seemed still a prospect of happiness for her when she and Mr. Cross went for a tour in Italy, settling, on their return, at her favourite country house at Witley. In the autumn they once more made their home in London, at Mr. Cross's town house at 4 Cheyne Walk, Chelsea, and Mrs. Cross, who was again beginning to receive her friends, seemed, to all appearances, well and happy, with a prospect of domestic love and unimpaired mental activity stretching out before her. But it was not to be. On Friday, the 17th of December, George Eliot attended a representation of the 'Agamemnon,' in Greek, by Oxford undergraduates, and was so stirred by the grand words of her favourite Æschylus, that she was contemplating a fresh perusal of the Greek dramatists with her husband. On the following day she went to the Saturday popular concert, and on returning home played through some of the music she had been hearing. Her fatal cold was probably caught on that occasion, for, although she received her friends, according to custom, on the Sunday afternoon, she felt indisposed in the evening, and on the following day an affection of the larynx necessitated medical advice. There seemed no cause for alarm at first, till on Wednesday it was unexpectedly discovered that inflammation had arisen in the heart, and that no hope of recovery remained. Before midnight of the 22nd of December, 1880, George Eliot, who died at precisely the same age as Lewes, had passed quietly and painlessly away; and on Christmas Eve the announcement of her death was

Q

received with general grief. She was buried by the side of George Henry Lewes, in the cemetery at Highgate.

George Eliot's career has been habitually described as uniform and uneventful. In reality nothing is more misleading. On the contrary, her life, from its rising to its setting, describes an astonishingly wide orbit. If one turns back in imagination from the little Staffordshire village whence her father sprang, to the simple rural surroundings of her own youth, and traces her history to the moment when a crowd of mourners, consisting of the most distinguished men and women in England, followed her to the grave, one cannot help realising how truly eventful was the life of her who now joined in spirit the

> " Choir invisible
> Of those immortal dead who live again
> In minds made better by their presence : live
> In pulses stirred to generosity,
> In deeds of daring rectitude, in scorn
> For miserable aims that end in self,
> In thoughts sublime that pierce the night like stars,
> And with their mild persistence urge man's search
> To vaster issues."

W. H. ALLEN & CO.'S PUBLICATIONS.

EMINENT WOMEN SERIES.

Edited by John H. Ingram.

Crown 8vo. 3s. 6d. each Volume.

VOLUMES ALREADY ISSUED:—

GEORGE ELIOT. By MATHILDE BLIND.

EMILY BRONTË. By A. MARY F. ROBINSON.

GEORGE SAND. By BERTHA THOMAS.

MARY LAMB. By ANNE GILCHRIST.

MARIA EDGEWORTH. By ELLEN ZIMMERN.

MARGARET FULLER. By JULIA WARD HOWE.

ELIZABETH FRY. By Mrs. E. R. PITMAN.

COUNTESS OF ALBANY. By VERNON LEE.

HARRIET MARTINEAU. By Mrs. FENWICK MILLER.

MARY WOLLSTONECRAFT GODWIN. By ELIZABETH ROBINS PENNELL.

RACHEL. By Mrs. A. KENNARD.

MADAME ROLAND. By MATHILDE BLIND.

SUSANNA WESLEY. By Mrs. CLARKE.

MARGARET OF ANGOULÊME, QUEEN OF NAVARRE. By A. MARY F. ROBINSON.

MRS. SIDDONS. By Mrs. KENNARD.

MADAME DE STAEL. By BELLA DUFFY.

HANNAH MORE. By CHARLOTTE M. YONGE.

ELIZABETH BARRETT BROWNING. By JOHN H. INGRAM.

Volume in Preparation.

JANE AUSTEN. By Mrs. MALDEN.

LONDON: W. H. ALLEN & CO., 13, WATERLOO PLACE, S.W.

W. H. ALLEN & CO.'S PUBLICATIONS.

THREE NEW NOVELS. Ready at all Libraries.

A MARTYR TO PRIDE. By WALTER STANHOPE. 1 vol.
Crown 8vo. 6s.

" It is a wild story. The romantic exuberance of the style, and the author's amusing disregard for truth to nature, make the story enjoyable in a way in which it was probably not meant to be."—*Scotsman.*

THE VOICE OF URBANO. A Romance of Adventure
on the Amazons. By J. W. WELLS, Author of " Three Thousand Miles through Brazil." 1 vol. Crown 8vo. 6s.

" A thoroughly healthy breezy romance of wild life, such as most of us have dreamed of, and a few experienced. . . . The book is full of exciting action. . . . All we can say in conclusion is that we mean to read ' The Voice of Urbano' over again."—*Academy.*

" This is a capital book for boys who have any love for adventure. It is a story of the Fenimore Cooper and Mayne Reid type."—*Whitehall Review.*

WALTER STANHOPE. By JOHN COPLAND. 1 vol.
Crown 8vo. 6s.

" The story is told in an unambitious straightforward manner, and the novel should find favour with those who enjoy a tale of quiet interest."—*Scotsman.*

COMO AND ITALIAN LAKE LAND. By T. W.
M. LUND, M.A., Chaplain to the School for the Blind, Liverpool. Crown 8vo. With 3 Maps, and 11 Illustrations by Miss Jessie Macgregor. 10s. 6d.

" The author is to be congratulated on having been aided by an illustrator of Miss Jessie Macgregor's talent. In a series of finely executed etchings she has portrayed many of the works of art, the sites, the types and costumes of the Italian Lake Land with rare fidelity."—*Morning Post.*

" It should certainly be in the hands of every intelligent tourist making a stay in or near the queen of Italian waters."—*Daily Telegraph.*

HANDBOOK OF THE ITALIAN SCHOOLS IN
THE DRESDEN GALLERY. By C. J. Ff. Crown 8vo. 3s. 6d.

" A useful compilation, both as a reference book for students and a guide for tourists. . . . There is a good index both to subjects and numbers."—*Saturday Review.*

" The book supplies a real want, and we hope that the author will find sufficient encouragement to induce her to extend the sphere of her useful and careful labour."—*Academy.*

SOME HOBBY-HORSES, AND HOW TO RIDE
THEM. By C. A. MONTRESOR. Crown 8vo. With Illustrations. 5s.

" Everybody who owns a scrap-book ought to read the instructive and gossipy essay, ' How to Keep a Scrap-book.' "—*Saturday Review.*

" An unusually pleasant little volume. It is simply a few pages of amusing gossip well fitted to lie about on the table, and be taken up at any leisure moment with the great probability that whoever does pick it up will speedily be retailing some unusually interesting scrap of information."—*Guardian.*

A LADY'S RANCHE LIFE IN MONTANA. By
I. R. Fcp. 8vo. 2s. 6d.

" The narrative is decidedly lively and amusing."—*Public Opinion.*

" Bright, chatty, and amusing letters."—*Morning Post.*

" A pleasant little book, compiled of lively diary notes, and ought to stimulate the young of both sexes in this effete country with delightful visions of emigration."—*Saturday Review.*

LONDON: W. H. ALLEN & Co., 13, Waterloo Place, S.W.

2

1509186R00122

Printed in Germany
by Amazon Distribution
GmbH, Leipzig